I0009788

Oracle Database 11g: SQL Fundamentals I

By

K. Lambercht

Copyright Notice

Table of Contents

Before you Start...

Before you start here are some Key features of the Oracle Database 11g: SQL Fundamentals I Certification Exam.

- ➢ The exam is Computer based and you have 120 minutes to answer 66 Questions.

- ➢ The Questions are (mostly) multiple choice type and there is NO penalty for an incorrect answer.

- ➢ You are not allowed to use any reference materials during the certification test (no access to online documentation or to any system).

- ➢ The Official Pass percentage is 60%. (This can vary slightly for your exam)

- ➢ In this book, unless otherwise stated, there is only one correct answer.

A Quick Quiz

Question: 1

What will be the result of following query?

SQL> SELECT TRUNC (ROUND (267.50,-1),-1) FROM DUAL;

A. 26
B. 267
C. 270
D. 267.50
E. 267.5

Answer: C

Explanation:

Round () function will execute initially and return 270 by rounding off "-1"position from right, which is 7. Therefore, value 267 will convert to 270. After rounding off, **Truncate ()** function will be used to remove all decimals and returns 270 as the final result.

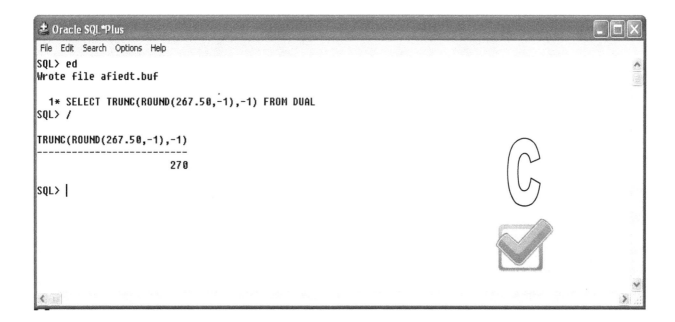

Question: 2

Which CREATE TABLE statement is valid?

A. CREATE TABLE order_detail
(ord_id NUMBER(2) PRIMARY KEY,
item_no NUMBER(3) PRIMARY KEY,
ord_date DATE NOT NULL);

B. CREATE TABLE order_detail
(ord_id NUMBER(2) UNIQUE, NOT NULL,
item_no NUMBER(3),
ord_date DATE DEFAULT SYSDATE NOT NULL);

C. CREATE TABLE order_detail
(ord_id NUMBER(2) ,
item_no NUMBER(3),
ord_date DATE DEFAULT NOT NULL,
CONSTRAINT ord_uq UNIQUE (ord_no),
CONSTRAINT ord_pk PRIMARY KEY (ord_id));

D. CREATE TABLE order_detail
(ord_id NUMBER(2),
item_no NUMBER(3),
ord_date DATE DEFAULT SYSDATE NOT NULL,
CONSTRAINT ord_pk PRIMARY KEY (ord_id, item_no));

Answer: D

Explanation:

In Oracle Database 11G, only single primary key is allowed in one table, therefore, answer "A" is invalid because two primary keys are defined there. In answer "B", there is a syntax error i.e. "unique" and "not null", as this should be written without comma. Option "C" is also invalid because default value against null is not defined in **order_date** column description.

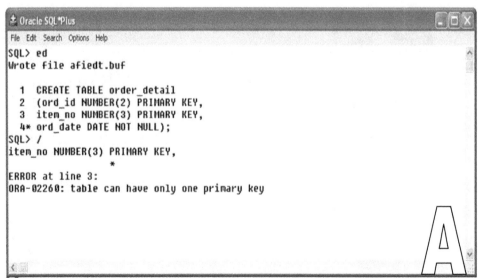

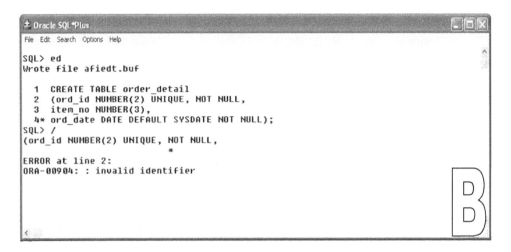

```
SQL> ed
Wrote file afiedt.buf

  1   CREATE TABLE order_detail
  2   (ord_id NUMBER(2) UNIQUE, NOT NULL,
  3   item_no NUMBER(3),
  4*  ord_date DATE DEFAULT SYSDATE NOT NULL);
SQL> /
(ord_id NUMBER(2) UNIQUE, NOT NULL,
                          *
ERROR at line 2:
ORA-00904: : invalid identifier
```
B

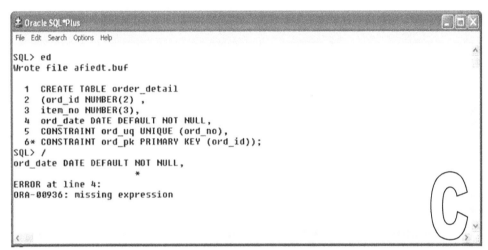

```
SQL> ed
Wrote file afiedt.buf

  1   CREATE TABLE order_detail
  2   (ord_id NUMBER(2) ,
  3   item_no NUMBER(3),
  4   ord_date DATE DEFAULT NOT NULL,
  5   CONSTRAINT ord_uq UNIQUE (ord_no),
  6*  CONSTRAINT ord_pk PRIMARY KEY (ord_id));
SQL> /
ord_date DATE DEFAULT NOT NULL,
                      *
ERROR at line 4:
ORA-00936: missing expression
```
C

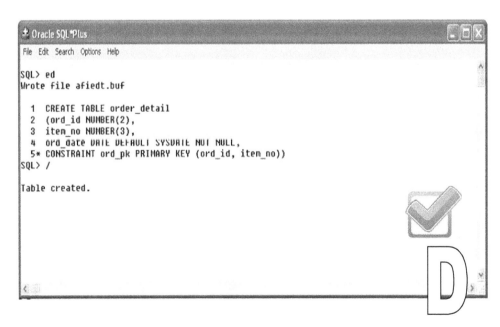

```
SQL> ed
Wrote file afiedt.buf

  1   CREATE TABLE order_detail
  2   (ord_id NUMBER(2),
  3   item_no NUMBER(3),
  4   ord_date DATE DEFAULT SYSDATE NOT NULL,
  5*  CONSTRAINT ord_pk PRIMARY KEY (ord_id, item_no))
SQL> /

Table created.
```
D

Question: 3

Following is the structure of the CUSTOMER_INFO table.

Column Name	I. /	Pk	Null?	Data Type
CUST_ID	1	1	N	NUMBER
FIRST_NAME	2		N	VARCHAR2 (20 Byte)
LAST_NAME	3		N	VARCHAR2 (20 Byte)
GENDER	4		N	CHAR (1 Byte)
YEAR_OF_BIRTH	5		Y	NUMBER (4)
MARITAL_STATUS	6		Y	VARCHAR2 (20 Byte)
STREET_ADDRESS	7		Y	VARCHAR2 (100 Byte)
POSTAL_CODE	8		Y	VARCHAR2 (10 Byte)
CITY	9		Y	VARCHAR2 (30 Byte)
STATE_PROVINCE	10		N	VARCHAR2 (40 Byte)
COUNTRY_ID	11		N	NUMBER
INCOME_LEVEL	12		Y	VARCHAR2 (30 Byte)
CUST_CREDIT_LIMIT	13		Y	NUMBER
EMAIL	14		Y	VARCHAR2 (100 Byte)

SCOTT.CUSTOMER_INFO — Show Navigator — Stay on top

Which of the following query will be used to find out the highest amount of customer credit limit in each city and in each income level

A) SELECT city, income_level, MAX(cust_credit_limit)
   FROM CUSTOMER_INFO
   GROUP BY city, income_level, cust_credit_limit;

B) SELECT city, income_level, MAX(cust_credit_limit)
   FROM CUSTOMER_INFO
   GROUP BY city, income_level;

C) SELECT city, income_level, MAX(cust_credit_limit)
   FROM CUSTOMER_INFO
   GROUP BY cust_credit_limit, income_level, city;

D) SELECT city, income_level, MAX(cust_credit_limit)
   FROM CUSTOMER_INFO
   GROUP BY city, income_level, MAX (cust_credit_limit);

Answer: B

Explanation: In option "A" field **cust_credit_limit** should not be a part of group by clause because it is not allowing the amount of credit limit to be sum. Option "C" has the same issue and three rows displayed as an output. Option "D" has an error because group by clause only allows single field name not group function.

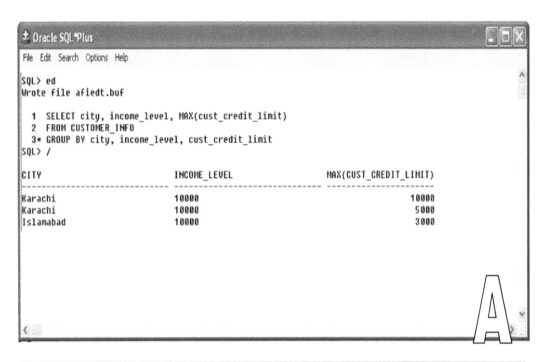

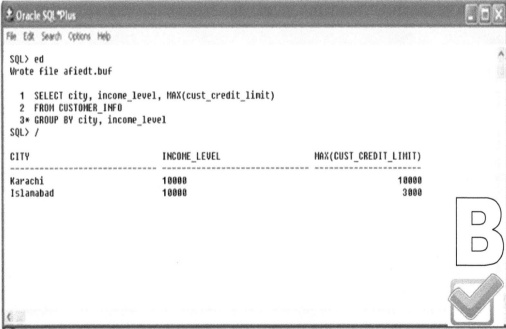

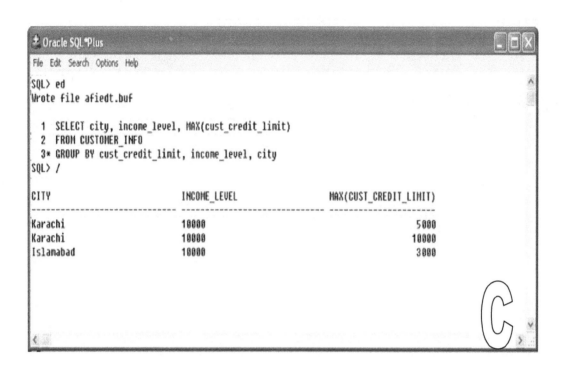

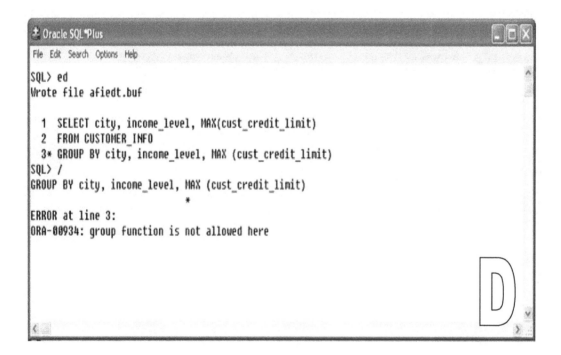

Question: 4

Which of the following CREATE TABLE statement is correct?

A. CREATE TABLE std9$# (temp_idNUMBER(4));
B. CREATE TABLE 9std$# (temp_idNUMBERS(4));
C. CREATE TABLE std*123 (temp_idNUMBER(4));
D. CREATE TABLE std9$# (temp_idNUMBER(4), date DATE);

Answer: A

Explanation: Option "B" is invalid because name of the table is starting from a numeric value, which is not allowed in Oracle 11G. Option "C" is also invalid because table name cannot contain reserved letters, such as, operators like '*' or' +'. In Option "D", word "**date**" is a reserved word in oracle 11g and cannot be used as a column name.

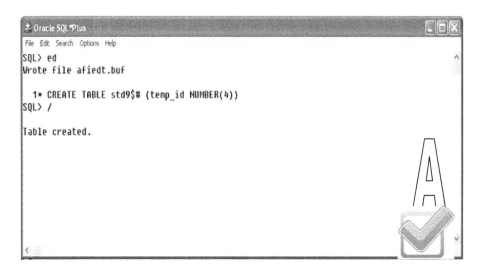

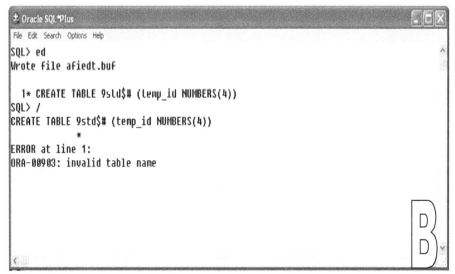

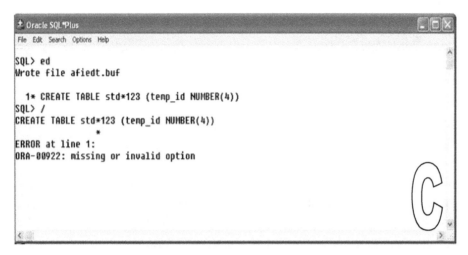

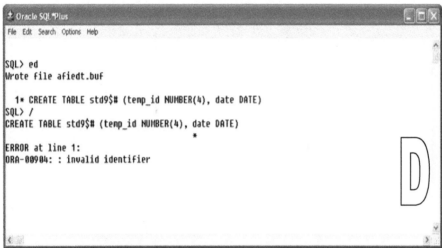

Question 5:

Have a look at the following data of PRODUCT_PRICE table:

PROD_ID	PROD_PRICE
123456	152525.99

What would be the outcome, if following query is executed?

```
SQL> SELECT LPAD((ROUND(prod_price)), 10,'*')
FROM product_price
WHERE prod_id = 123456;
```

A. *15252****
B. ****152526
C. 152525**
D. an error message

Answer: B

Explanation: In first step, value of "**prod_price**" will be rounded off. As a result, all decimals will be removed and 152526 will be the output. After that, **LPAD ()** function will add additional four "*" characters to make the pad count to 10.

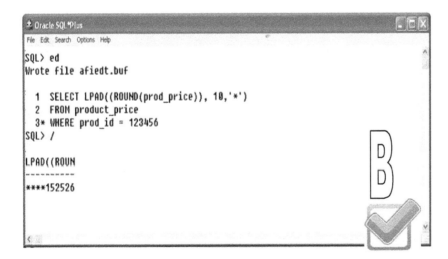

Question: 6

Following is the structure and data of CUSTOMER table. After execution which of the following statement is true?

SQL> SELECT CUST_ID, NVL2 (NULLIF(spent_amt, limit), 0, 2000)"Inc_AMT"
FROM customer;

Column Name	ID	Pk	Null?	Data Type
CUST_ID	1	Y	Y	NUMBER
> SPENT_AMT	2		Y	NUMBER
LIMIT	3		Y	NUMBER

CUST_ID	SPENT_AMT	LIMIT
1	1000	1000
2	2000	2500
3		3000
4	4000	2800

A. It produces an error because the SPENT_AMT column contains a null value
B. It displays an Increment of 2000 for all customers whose SPENT_AMT is less than their LIMIT.
C. It displays an Increment of 2000 for all customers whose SPENT_AMT is equals to LIMIT.
D. It produces an error.

Answer: C

Explanation: NULLIF () function returns null value when both field values in this function are same and it returns value of first field when both field value are not same.

Here, the first field is **"amt_spent"** and second value is **"credit limit"** considering first row, both value are same i.e. "1000" so it will return null as the output and so on.

Finally output will look as follows:

2000
4000

Now, outer query **NVL2 ()** will return 2000, if incoming value is NULL or returns 0 when row is not NULL

So it places 2000 at first and third position.

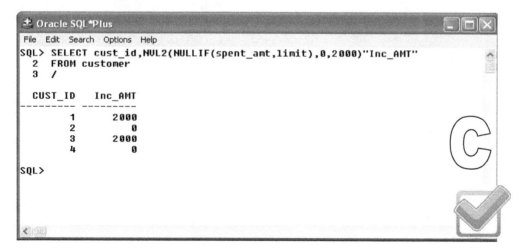

Question: 7

Which query will be used to find out the number of days from 1st January 2014 till date?

A. SELECT SYSDATE - '01-JAN-2014' FROM DUAL;
B. SELECT SYSDATE - TO_DATE ('01/JANUARY/2014') FROM DUAL;
C. SELECT TO_CHAR (SYSDATE, 'DD-MON-YYYY') - '01-JAN-2014' FROM DUAL;
D. SELECT SYSDATE - TO_DATE ('01-JANUARY-2014') FROM DUAL;
E. SELECT TO_DATE (SYSDATE, 'DD/MONTH/YYYY') - '01/JANUARY/2014' FROM DUAL;

Answer: B, D

Explanation: In Option "A", data type of **sysdate** is **date,** while **'01-JAN-2014'** has a **character** data type. Therefore, subtraction cannot be done between data and character.

In the same way, in option "C" TO_CHAR(SYSDATE, 'DD-MON-YYYY') returns **character** type value and '01-JAN-2014' is also a **character** value so subtraction between both characters are not allowed.

Aslo, in option "E", **date** type value minus **character** type value has made this option invalid.

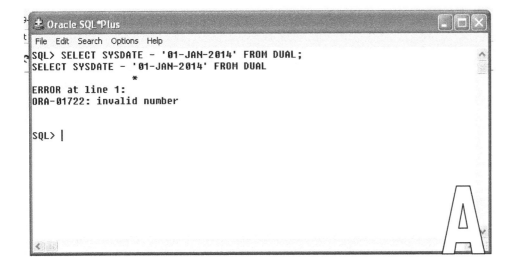

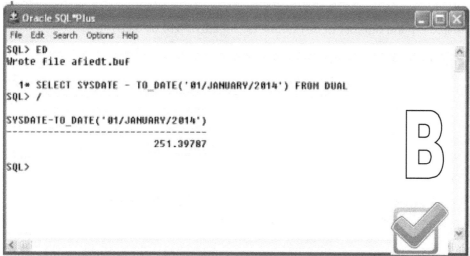

```
Oracle SQL*Plus
File Edit Search Options Help
SQL> ED
Wrote file afiedt.buf

  1* SELECT SYSDATE - TO_DATE('01/JANUARY/2014') FROM DUAL
SQL> /

SYSDATE-TO_DATE('01/JANUARY/2014')
----------------------------------
                         251.39787

SQL>
```

B ✓

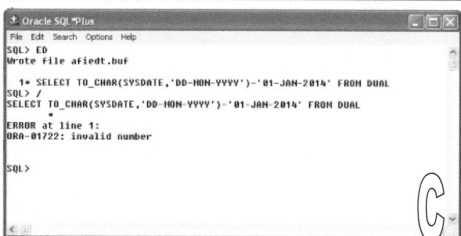

```
Oracle SQL*Plus
File Edit Search Options Help
SQL> ED
Wrote file afiedt.buf

  1* SELECT TO_CHAR(SYSDATE,'DD-MON-YYYY')-'01-JAN-2014' FROM DUAL
SQL> /
SELECT TO_CHAR(SYSDATE,'DD-MON-YYYY')-'01-JAN-2014' FROM DUAL
       *
ERROR at line 1:
ORA-01722: invalid number

SQL>
```

C

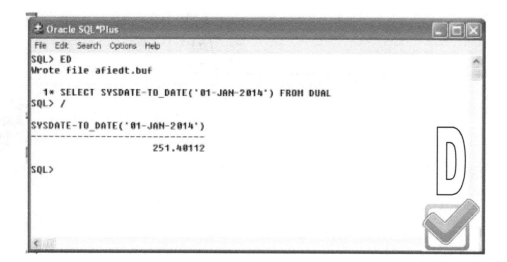

```
Oracle SQL*Plus
File Edit Search Options Help
SQL> ED
Wrote file afiedt.buf

  1* SELECT SYSDATE-TO_DATE('01-JAN-2014') FROM DUAL
SQL> /

SYSDATE-TO_DATE('01-JAN-2014')
------------------------------
                     251.40112

SQL>
```

D ✓

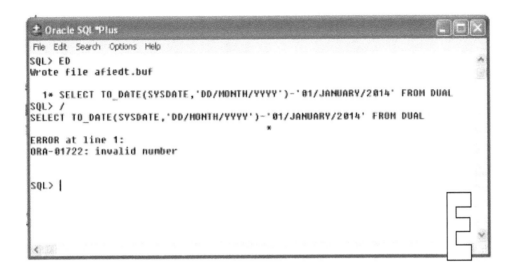

Question: 8

Examine the structure of the INVOICE table.

Column Name	ID	Pk	Null?	Data Type
▶ INVOICE_ID	1		N	NUMBER
IN_DATE	2		Y	DATE
AMOUNT	3		Y	NUMBER

Which two SQL statements would execute successfully?

A. SELECT INVOICE_ID, NVL2 (IN_DATE,'INPROGRESS','COMPLETE')
        FROM INVOICE;
B. SELECT INVOICE_ID, NVL2 (AMOUNT, IN_DATE,'NOT DEFINE')
        FROM INVOICE;
C. SELECT INVOICE_ID, NVL2 (IN_DATE, SYSDATE - IN_DATE, SYSDATE)
        FROM INVOICE;
D. SELECT INVOICE_ID, NVL2 (AMOUNT, AMOUNT *.75,'NOT DEFINE')
        FROM INVOICE;

Answer: A, C

Explanation: NVL2 () function returns the value of the same data type on which **NVL ()** has applied. Option "B" will not execute because **NVL2 ()** has applied on "**Amount**" field which is **numeric,** while the return value of "**Not Define**" is a **character**. Same issue exist with option "D" where Data type "**Amount*.75**" and "**Not Define**" are not same

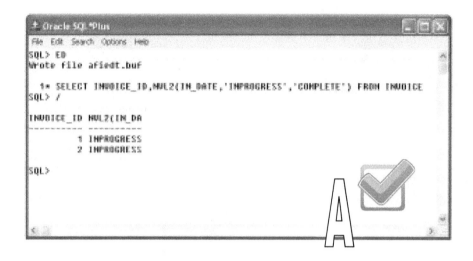

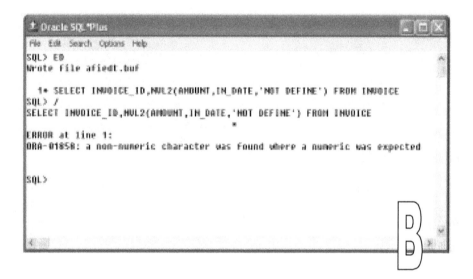

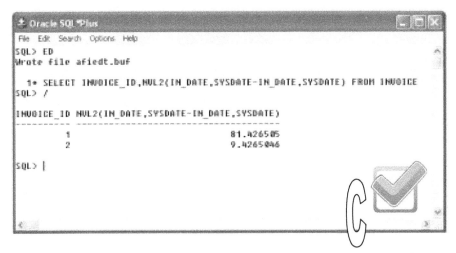

Question: 9

Which statement is true regarding the below query?

SQL>SELECT cust_id, last_name
FROM customer_info
WHERE cust_credit_limit IN
(select cust_credit_limit
FROM customer_info
WHERE city ='Karachi');

A. It produces an error.
B. It executes with 0 rows.

C. It generates output for NULL with result from sub query.
D. This query ignores the NULL value and only display result from sub query.

Answer: D

Explanation: Sub query will return **cust_credit_limit** for those customers who are from Karachi City. Main query will return those customers whose credit limit is same as sub query.

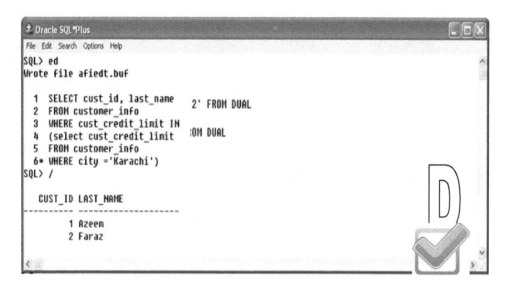

Question: 10

To display the date **07-Sep-2014** in words ('Seventh of September, Twenty Fourteen').-

Which query will provide the desired output?

A. SELECT TO CHAR ('07-Sep-2014', 'fmDdspth "of" Month, Year')
    FROM DUAL;
B. SELECT TO_CHAR (TO_DATE('07-Sep-2014'), 'fmDdspth of month, year')
    FROM DUAL;
C. SELECT TO_CHAR (TO_DATE('07-Sep-2014'), 'fmDdspth "of" Month, Year')
    FROM DUAL;
D. SELECT TO_DATE (TO_CHAR('07-Sep-2014','fmDdspth "of" Month, Year'))
    FROM DUAL;

Answer: C

Explanation: Option "A" is not correct because **to_char ()** function with format mask cannot be applied on character value.

In option "B" word '**of**' must enclose in double quotes because '**of** 'is not a part of format mask and must be written in double quotes to make format mask valid.

Option "D" is invalid because **to_char ()** function cannot be applied on character '**11-oct-2009**' value with format mask.

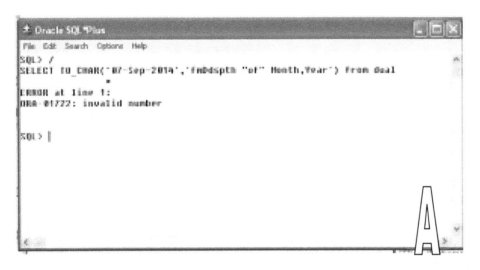

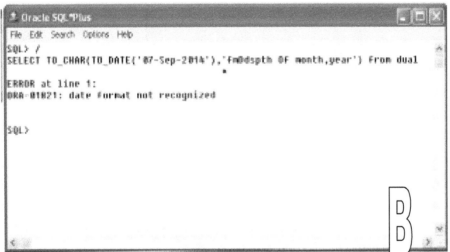

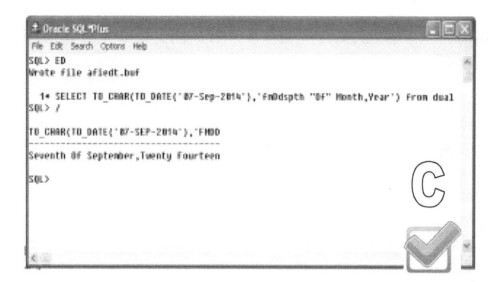

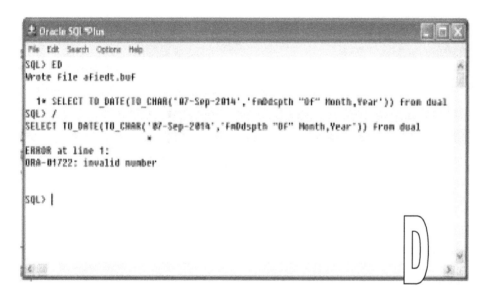

ORACLE DATABASE ADMISTRATOR; SQL Fundamentals

1. **Which operator will be evaluated first in the following SELECT statement?**
   SELECT (2+3*4/2–5) FROM dual;

   a) +
   b) *
   c) /
   d) –

   Answer: b

   Explanation:

   In the arithmetic operators, unary operators are evaluated first, then multiplication and division, and finally addition and subtraction. The expression is evaluated from left to right.

   Illustration:

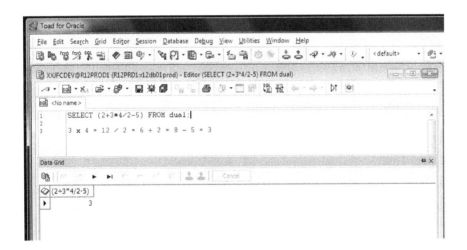

2. **Which one of the following statements is true?**

   a) A view can be created before creating the base table.
   b) A view cannot be created before creating the base table.
   c) A view will not become invalid if the base table's column referred to in the view is altered.
   d) A view will become invalid if any column in the base table is altered.

   Answer: a

Explanation:

The CREATE FORCE VIEW statement can be used to create a view before its base table is created. In versions prior to Oracle 11g, any modification to the table will invalidate the view. In Oracle 11g, the view will be invalidated only if the columns used in the view are modified in the base table. Use the ALTER VIEW <view name> COMPILE statement to recompile the view.

3. **Which function can return a non-NULL value if passed a NULL argument?**

a) NULLIF
b) LENGTH
c) CONCAT
d) INSTR

Answer: c

Explanation:

CONCAT will return a non-NULL if only one parameter is NULL. Both CONCAT parameters would need to be NULL for CONCAT to return NULL. The NULLIF function returns NULL if the two parameters are equal. The LENGTH of a NULL is NULL. INSTR will return NULL if NULL is passed in and the tangent of a NULL is NULL.

4. **The following statement will raise an exception on which line?**

```
select dept_name, avg(all salary)
,count(*) "number of employees"
from emp , dept
where deptno = dept_no
and count(*) > 5
group by dept_name
order by 2 desc;
```

a) select dept_name, avg(all salary), count(*) "number of employees"
b) where deptno = dept_no
c) and count(*) > 5
d) group by dept_name
e) order by 2 desc;

Answer: c

Explanation:

Group functions cannot appear in the WHERE clause.

Illustration:

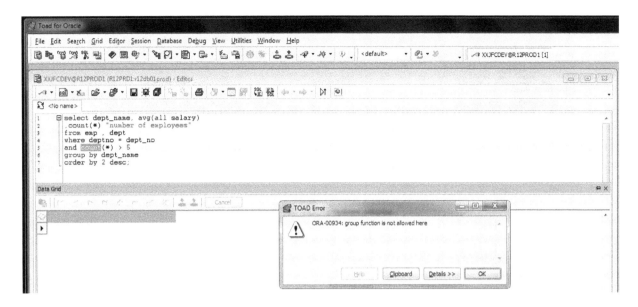

5. **Review the code segment. Which line has an error?**

    1 INSERT INTO salaries VALUES (101, 23400, SYSDATE);
    2 UPDATE salaries
    3 SET salary = salary * 1.1
    4 AND effective_dt = SYSDATE
    5 WHERE empno = 333;

    a) 2
    b) 4
    c) 5
    d) There is no error.

    Answer: b

    Explanation:

    When updating multiple columns in a single UPDATE statement, the column assignments in the SET
    clause must be separated by commas, not AND operators.

    Illustration:
    After running the SQL script.

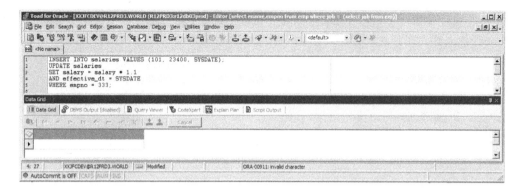

6. **Review the following SQL, and choose the most appropriate option.**

    SELECT job, COUNT(*)
    FROM employees
    GROUP BY deptno;

    a) The statement will show the number of jobs in each department.
    b) The statement will show the number of employees in each department.
    c) The statement will generate an error.
    d) The statement will work if the GROUP BY clause is removed.

    Answer: c

    Explanation:

    Since job is used in the SELECT clause, it must be used in the GROUP BY clause.
    Illustration:

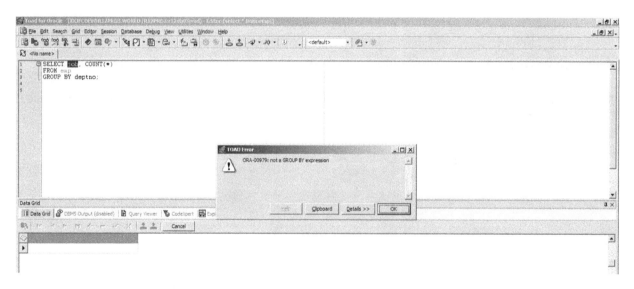

7. **Which datatype stores data outside Oracle Database?**

a) UROWID
b) BFILE
c) BLOB
d) NCLOB
e) EXTERNAL

Answer: b

Explanation:

The BFILE datatype stores only the locator to an external file in the database; the actual data is stored as an operating system file. BLOB, NCLOB, and CLOB are the other large object data types in Oracle 11g. UROWID is Universal ROWID datatype and EXTERNAL is a not a valid datatype.

8. **The DEPT table has the following data:**

SQL> SELECT * FROM dept;

```
DEPTNO  DNAME        LOC
------  -----------  ----------
10      ACCOUNTING   NEW YORK
20      RESEARCH     DALLAS
30      SALES        CHICAGO
40      OPERATIONS   BOSTON
```

Consider this INSERT statement, and choose the best answer:

INSERT INTO (SELECT * FROM dept WHERE deptno = 10)
VALUES (50, 'MARKETING', 'FORT WORTH');

a) The INSERT statement is invalid; a valid table name is missing.
b) 50 is not a valid DEPTNO value, since the subquery limits DEPTNO to 10.
c) The statement will work without error.
d) A subquery and a VALUES clause cannot appear together.

Answer: c

Explanation:

The statement will work without error. Option b would be correct if you used the WITH CHECK OPTION clause in the subquery.

Illustration:

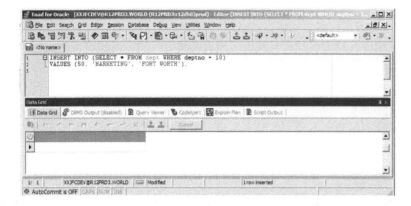

9. **Which two of the following queries are valid syntax that would return all rows from the EMP and DEPT tables, even if there are no corresponding/related rows in the other table?**

   a) SELECT ename, dname
      FROM emp e FULL JOIN dept d
      ON e.deptno = d.deptno;

   b) SELECT ename, dname
      FROM emp e OUTER JOIN dept d
      ON e.deptno = d.deptno;

   c) SELECT e.ename, d.dname
      FROM emp e
      LEFT OUTER JOIN dept d
      ON e.deptno = d.deptno
      RIGHT OUTER JOIN emp f
      ON f.deptno = d.deptno;

   d) SELECT e.ename, d.dname
      FROM emp e
      CROSS JOIN dept d
      ON e.deptno = d.deptno;

Answer: a

Explanation:

An outer join on both tables can be achieved using the FULL OUTER JOIN syntax. You can specify the join condition using the ON clause to specify the columns explicitly or using the USING clause to specify the columns with common column names. Options b and d would result in errors. In option b, the join type is not specified; OUTER is an optional keyword. In option d, CROSS JOIN is used to get a Cartesian result, and Oracle does not expect a join condition.

Illustration:

Option a

Option b

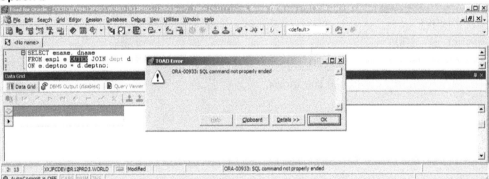

Option c

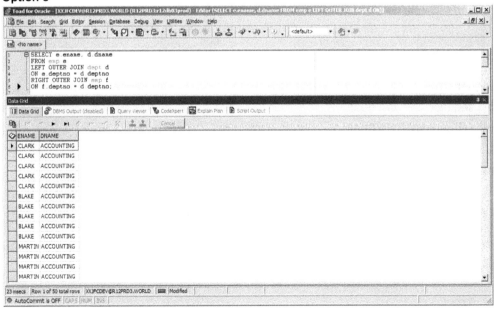

Option d

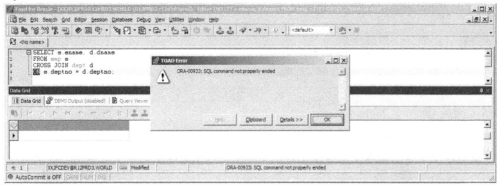

10. Which of the following statements could use an index on the columns PRODUCT_ID and WAREHOUSE_ID of the OE.INVENTORIES table? (Choose all that apply.)

a) select count(distinct warehouse_id) from oe.inventories;

b) select product_id, quantity_on_hand

from oe.inventories

where product_id = 100;

c) insert into oe.inventories values (5,100,32);

d) None of these statements could use the index.

Answer: a and b

Explanation:

a, b. The index contains all the information needed to satisfy the query in option a, and a full-index scan would be faster than a full-table scan. A subset of index columns is specified in the WHERE clause of option b; hence, Oracle 11g can use the index.

11. **The following statements are executed:**

create sequence my_seq;

select my_seq.nextval from dual;

select my_seq.nextval from dual;

rollback;

select my_seq.nextval from dual;

What value will be returned when the last SQL SELECT statement is executed?

a) 0

b) 1

c) 2

d) 3

Answer: d

Explanation:

The CREATE SEQUENCE statement will create an increasing sequence that will start with 1, will increment by 1, and will be unaffected by the rollback. A rollback will never stuff vales back into a sequence.

Illustration:

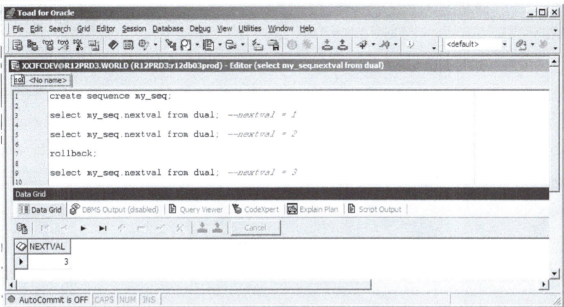

12. **Which of the following statements are true? (Choose two.)**

    a) Primary key constraints allow NULL values in the columns.
    b) Unique key constraints allow NULL values in the columns.
    c) Primary key constraints do not allow NULL values in the columns.
    d) A non-unique index cannot be used to enforce primary key constraints.

    Answer: b and c

    Explanation:

    Primary and unique key constraints can be enforced using non-unique indexes. Unique constraints allow NULL values in the columns, but primary keys do not.

13. **The current time in Dubai is 04-APR-2008 08:50:00, and the time in Dallas is 03-APR-2008 23:50:00. A user from Dubai is connected to a session in the database located on a server in Dallas. What will be the result of his query?**

SELECT TO_CHAR(SYSDATE,'DD-MON-YYYY HH24:MI:SS') FROM dual;

a) 04-APR-2008 08:50:00
b) 03-APR-2008 23:50:00
c) 03-APR-2008 2324:50:00
d) None of the above

Answer: b

Explanation:

The **SYSDATE** function returns the date and time on the server where the database instance is started. **CURRENT_DATE** returns the local date and time.

14. **The DEPT table has the following structure:**

DEPTNO (4)
DNAME
LOC

How many rows will be counted from the last SQL statement in the code segment?

SELECT COUNT(*) FROM DEPT;

COUNT(*)

4

```
INSERT INTO DEPT VALUES (50, 'MARKETING', 'NEW JERSEY', null);

SAVEPOINT A

INSERT INTO DEPT VALUES (60, 'INFO MNGT', 'LOS ANGELES', null);

SAVEPOINT B

INSERT INTO DEPT VALUES (70, 'SUPPLY CHAIN', 'CHICAGO', null);

ROLLBACK TO A;

INSERT INTO DEPT VALUES (80, 'WAREHOUSE', 'TEXAS', null);

COMMIT;

SELECT COUNT (*) FROM DEPT;
```

a) 7
b) 4
c) 5
d) 6

Answer: d

Explanation:

The first INSERT statement and last INSERT statement will be saved in the database. The ROLLBACK TO A statement will undo the second and third inserts.

Illustration:

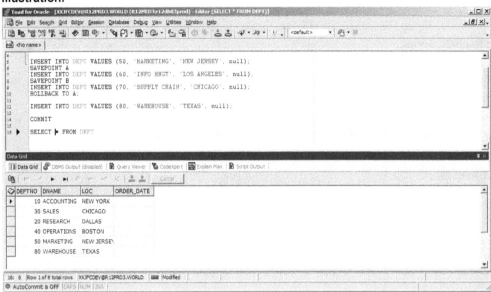

15. At a minimum, how many join conditions should be there to avoid a Cartesian join if there are three tables in the FROM clause?

a) 1
b) 2
c) 3
d) There is no minimum.

Answer: d

Explanation:

There should be at least n-1 join conditions when joining n tables to avoid a Cartesian join.

16. **Why does the following statement fail?**

CREATE TABLE FRUITS-N-VEGETABLES
(NAME VARCHAR2 (40));

a) The table should have more than one column in its definition.
b) NAME is a reserved word, which cannot be used as a column name.
c) Oracle does not like the table name.
d) The column length cannot exceed 30 characters.

Answer: c

Explanation:

The table and column names can include only three special characters: #, $, and _. No other characters are allowed in the table name. You can have letters and numbers in the table name.

Illustration:
After running the SQL Script.

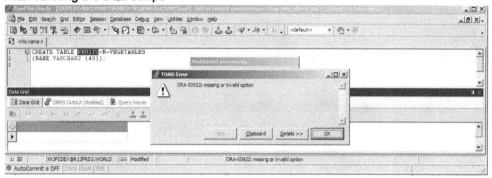

17. Which two statements are true about NULL values?

    a) You cannot search for a NULL value in a column using the WHERE clause.
    b) If a NULL value is returned in the subquery or if NULL is included in the list when using
    c) NOT IN operator, no rows will be returned.
    d) In an ascending-order sort, NULL values appear at the bottom of the result set.

    Answer: b

    Explanation:

    You can use the IS NULL or IS NOT NULL operator to search for NULLs or non-NULLs in a column. Since NULLs are sorted higher, they appear at the bottom of the result set in an ascending-order sort.

18. Table CUSTOMERS has a column named CUST_ZIP that could be NULL. Which of the following functions include the NULL rows in its result?

    a) COUNT (CUST_ZIP)
    b) SUM (CUST_ZIP)
    c) AVG (DISTINCT CUST_ZIP)
    d) None of the above

    Answer: d

    Explanation:

COUNT (<column_name>) does not include the NULL values, whereas COUNT (*) includes the NULL values. No other aggregate function takes NULL into consideration.

19. Using the following EMP table, you need to increase everyone's salary by 5 percent of their combined salary and bonus. Which of the following statements will achieve the desired results?

Column Name emp_id name salary bonus
Key Type pk pk
NULLs/Unique NN NN NN
FK Table
Datatype VARCHAR2 VARCHAR2 NUMBER NUMBER
Length 9 50 11,2 11,2

a) `UPDATE emp SET sal = (sal + comm)*1.05;`
b) `UPDATE emp SET sal = sal * 1.05 + comm * 1.05;`
c) `UPDATE emp SET sal = sal + (sal + comm)*0.05;`
d) None of these statements will achieve the desired results.

Answer: d

Explanation:

These statements don't account for possible NULL values in the BONUS column.

Illustration:
Given:

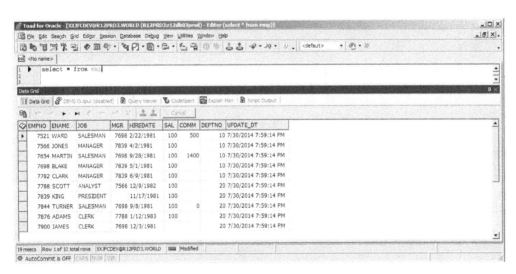

Option a – Result using `UPDATE emp SET sal = (sal + comm)*1.05;`

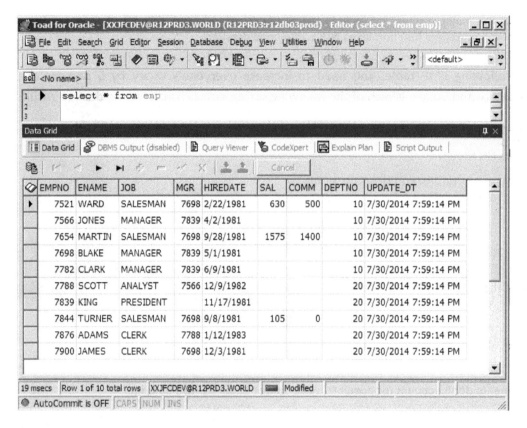

Option b – Result using `UPDATE emp SET sal = sal * 1.05 + comm * 1.05;`

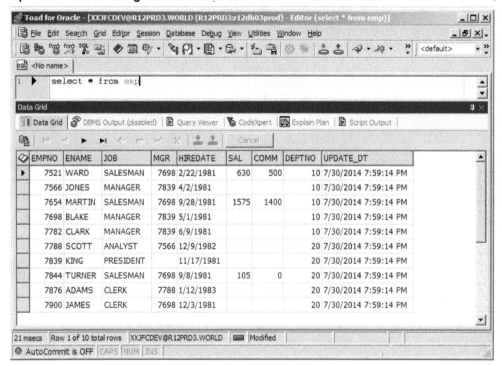

Option c – Result using `UPDATE emp SET sal = sal + (sal + comm)*0.05;`

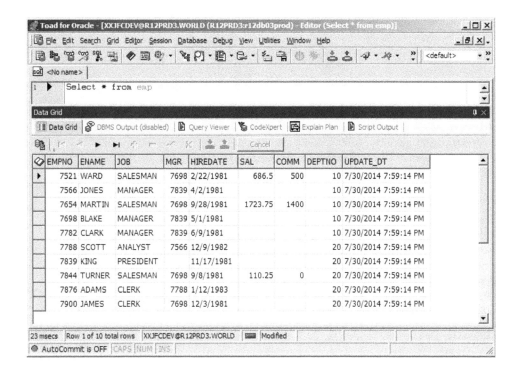

20. You need to change employees in DEPTNO 10 who have a JOB of 'MANAGER' and ENAME of 'CLARK' to DEPTNO 40 and to MGR 7840. Which option will best satisfy these requirements using below data?

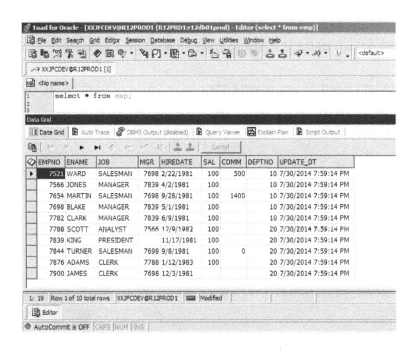

a)
```
UPDATGE EMP
SET DEPTNO = 10
AND MGR = 7840
```

```
    WHERE DEPTNO = 10
    AND JOB = 'MANAGER'
    AND ENAME = 'CLARK';
```

b) UPDATE EMP
```
    SET (DEPTNO, MGR) = (30, 7840)
    WHERE DEPTNO = 10
    AND JOB = 'MANAGER'
    AND ENAME = 'CLARK';
```

c) UPDATGE EMP
```
    SET DEPTNO = 10
    ,MGR = 7840
    WHERE DEPTNO = 10
    AND JOB = 'MANAGER'
    AND ENAME = 'CLARK';
```

d) You need to use two UPDATE statements: one for DEPARTMENT_ID and one for MANAGER_ID.

Answer: c

Explanation:

Option a is wrong because of AND statement used in defining compound or multiple column to update. Comma (",") should be used instead of AND.

Option b is wrong because of ORA-01767: UPDATE ... SET expression must be a subquery.

Option d is wrong because you don't need to use update statement twice to update the two(2) columns.

Illustration:

Option a

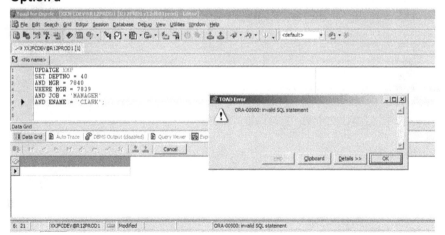

Option b

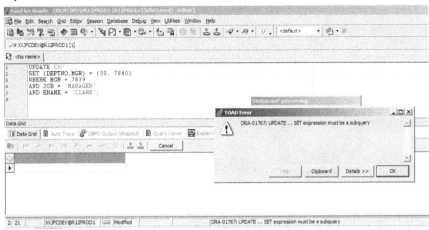

Option c

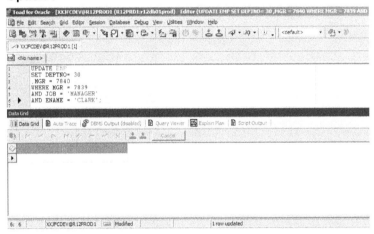

21. **Which option is not available in Oracle when modifying tables?**

a) Adding new columns
b) Renaming existing columns
c) Dropping existing columns
d) None of the above

Answer: d

Explanation:

Using the **ALTER TABLE** statement, you can add new columns, rename existing columns, and drop existing columns.

Illustration:

ADD MULTIPLE COLUMNS IN TABLE

SYNTAX

To **ADD MULTIPLE COLUMNS** to an existing table, the Oracle ALTER TABLE syntax is:

```
ALTER TABLE table_name
  ADD (column_1 column-definition,
       column_2 column-definition,
       ...
       column_n column_definition);
```

MODIFY COLUMN IN TABLE

SYNTAX

To **MODIFY A COLUMN** in an existing table, the Oracle ALTER TABLE syntax is:

```
ALTER TABLE table_name
  MODIFY column_name column_type;
```

MODIFY MULTIPLE COLUMNS IN TABLE

SYNTAX

To **MODIFY MULTIPLE COLUMNS** in an existing table, the Oracle ALTER TABLE syntax is:

```
ALTER TABLE table_name
  MODIFY (column_1 column_type,
          column_2 column_type,
          ...
          column_n column_type);
```

DROP COLUMN IN TABLE

SYNTAX

To **DROP A COLUMN** in an existing table, the Oracle ALTER TABLE syntax is:

```
ALTER TABLE table_name
  DROP COLUMN column_name;
```

RENAME COLUMN IN TABLE
(NEW IN ORACLE 9I RELEASE 2)

SYNTAX

Starting in Oracle 9i Release 2, you can now rename a column.

To **RENAME A COLUMN** in an existing table, the Oracle ALTER TABLE syntax is:

```
ALTER TABLE table_name
  RENAME COLUMN old_name to new_name;
```

RENAME TABLE

SYNTAX

To **RENAME A TABLE**, the Oracle ALTER TABLE syntax is:

```
ALTER TABLE table_name
  RENAME TO new_table_name;
```

22. **The following data is from the EMPLOYEES table:**

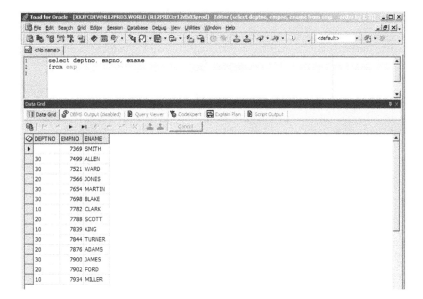

Which EMPNO will be returned last when the following query is executed?

select deptno, empno, ename
from emp
order by 1, 2

a)   7499
b)   7369
c)   7521
d)   7934

Answer: b

Explanation:

Since DEPARTMENT_ID is NULL for employee 7369, NULL will be sorted after the non-NULL values when doing an ascending-order sort. Since I did not specify the sort order or the NULLS FIRST clause, the defaults are ASC and NULLS LAST.

Illustration:

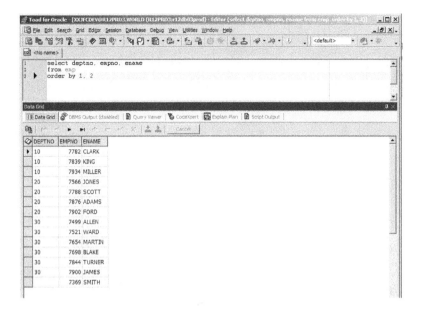

23. INTERVAL datatypes store a period of time. Which components are included in the INTERVAL DAY TO SECOND datatype column? (Choose one that does not apply.)

a) Days
b) Hours
c) Minutes
d) Fractional seconds

Answer: d

Explanation:

The INTERVAL DAY TO SECOND datatype is used to store an interval between two datetime components.

Illustration:

```
SQL> CREATE TABLE t1 (c1 INTERVAL DAY(5) TO SECOND(3));

Table created.

SQL> INSERT INTO t1 VALUES (TO_DSINTERVAL('2 10:20:30.456'));

1 row created.
```

```
SQL> SELECT * FROM t1;
C1
---------------------
+00002 10:20:30.456
```

24. The primary key of the STATE table is STATE_CD. The primary key of the CITY table is STATE_CD/CITY_CD. The STATE_CD column of the CITY table is the foreign key to the STATE table. There are no other constraints on these two tables. Consider the following view definition:

CREATE OR REPLACE VIEW state_city AS
SELECT a.state_cd, a.state_name, b.city_cd, b.city_name

FROM state a, city b
WHERE a.state_cd = b.state_cd;

Which of the following operations are permitted on the base tables of the view? (Choose one that apply.)

a) Insert a record into the CITY table.
b) Insert a record into the STATE table.
c) Update the STATE_CD column of the CITY table.
d) Update the CITY_CD column of the CITY table.

Answer: d

Explanation:

In the join view, CITY is the key-preserved table. You can update the columns of the CITY table, except STATE_CD, because STATE_CD is not part of the view definition (the STATE_CD column in the view is from the STATE table). Since I did not include the STATE_CD column from the CITY table, no INSERT operations are permitted (STATE_CD is part of the primary key). If the view were defined as follows, all the columns of the CITY table would have been updatable, and new records could be inserted into the CITY table.

```
CREATE OR REPLACE VIEW state_city AS
SELECT b.state_cd, a.state_name, b.city_cd, b.city_name
FROM states a, cities b
WHERE a.state_cd = b.state_cd;
```

25. **The table EMP has the following data:**

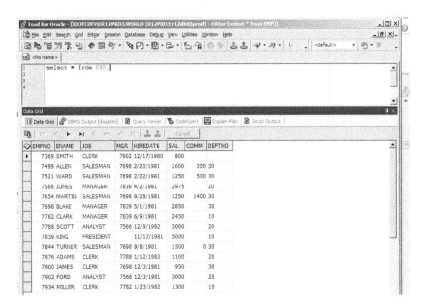

You issue the following command to alter the table. Which line of code will cause an error?

1 ALTER TABLE EMP
2 MODIFY

3 (HIREDATE DEFAULT SYSDATE NOT NULL,
4 DEPTNP NOT NULL);

a) Line 2 will cause an error.
b) Line 3 will cause an error.
c) Line 4 will cause an error.
d) There will be no error.

Answer: c

Explanation:

When altering an existing column to add a NOT NULL constraint, no rows in the table should have NULL values. In the example, there are two rows with NULL values.

Illustration:

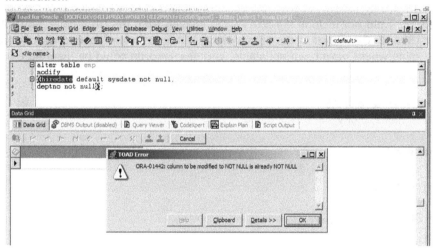

26. In ANSI SQL, a self-join can be represented by using which of the following? (Choose the best answer.)

a) NATURAL JOIN clause
b) CROSS JOIN clause
c) JOIN...USING clause
d) JOIN...ON clause

Answer: d

Explanation:

NATURAL JOIN and JOIN...USING clauses will not allow alias names to be used. Since a self-join is getting data from the same table, you must include alias names and qualify column names.

Illustration:

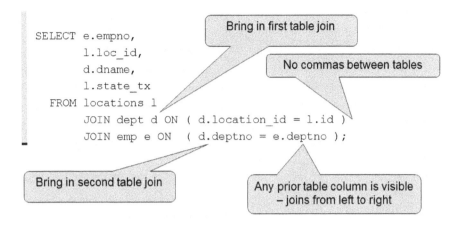

```
SELECT e.empno,
       l.loc_id,
       d.dname,
       l.state_tx
  FROM locations l
       JOIN dept d ON ( d.location_id = l.id )
       JOIN emp e ON  ( d.deptno = e.deptno );
```

Bring in first table join

No commas between tables

Bring in second table join

Any prior table column is visible – joins from left to right

27. **What will be result of trunc(2916.16, -1)?**

a) 2916.2
b) 290
c) 2916.1
d) 2910

Answer: d

Explanation:

The TRUNC function used with a negative second argument will truncate to the left of the decimal.

Illustration:

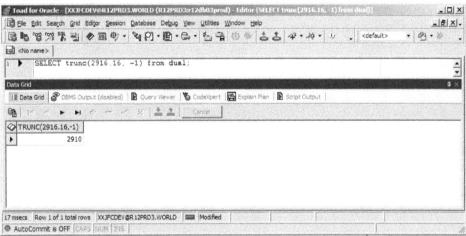

28. **The table ADDRESSES is created using the following syntax. How many indexes will be created automatically when this table is created?**

```
CREATE TABLE ADDRESSES (
NAME VARCHAR2 (40) PRIMARY KEY,
STREET VARCHAR2 (40),
CITY VARCHAR2 (40),
```

```
STATE CHAR (2),
ZIP NUMBER (5) NOT NULL,
PHONE VARCHAR2 (12) UNIQUE);
```

a) 0

b) 1

c) 2

d) 3

Answer: c

Explanation:

Oracle creates unique indexes for each unique key and primary key defined in the table. The table **ADDRESSES** has one unique key and a primary key. Indexes will not be created for NOT NULL or foreign key constraints.

Illustration:

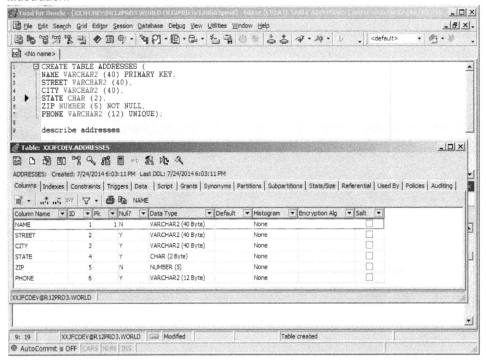

29. **Which line of the following code has an error?**

```
SELECT *
FROM emp
WHERE comm = NULL
ORDER BY ename;
```

a) SELECT *

b) FROM emp

c) WHERE comm = NULL

d) There is no error in this statement.

Answer: d

Explanation:

Although there is no error in this statement, the statement will not return the desired result. When a NULL is compared, you cannot use the = or != operator; you must use the IS NULL or IS NOT NULL operator.

Illustration:

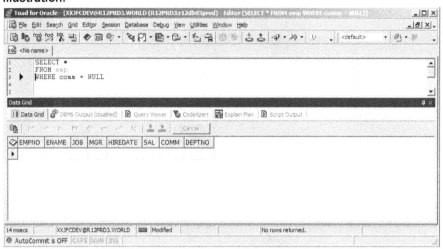

30. **Which of the following statements will raise an exception?**

   a) alter sequence emp_seq nextval 23050;
   b) alter sequence emp_seq nocycle;
   c) alter sequence emp_seq increment by -5;
   d) alter sequence emp_seq maxvalue 10000;

Answer: a

Explanation:

You cannot explicitly change the next value of a sequence. You can set the MAXVALUE or INCREMENT BY value to a negative number, and NOCYCLE tells Oracle to not reuse a sequence number.

Illustration:

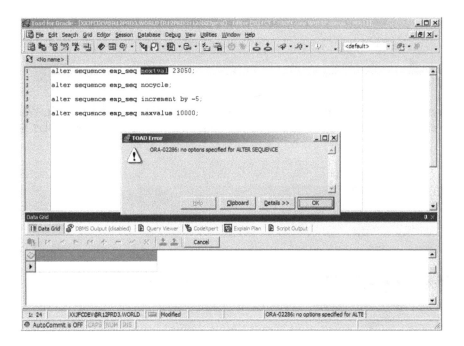

31. What order does Oracle use in resolving a table or view referenced in a SQL statement?

a) Table/view within user's schema, public synonym, private synonym
b) Table/view within user's schema, private synonym, public synonym
c) Public synonym, table/view within user's schema, private synonym
d) Private synonym, public synonym, table/view within user's schema

Answer: b

Explanation:

The following example illustrates how Oracle resolves references to objects within SQL statements.

Consider this statement that adds a row of data to a table identified by the name departments:

INSERT INTO departments VALUES (280, 'ENTERTAINMENT_CLERK', 206, 1700);

Based on the context of the statement, Oracle determines that departments can be:

A table in your own schema
A view in your own schema
A private synonym for a table or view
A public synonym

Oracle always attempts to resolve an object reference within the namespaces in your own schema before considering namespaces outside your schema. In this example, Oracle attempts to resolve the name departments as follows:

1. First, Oracle attempts to locate the object in the namespace in your own schema containing tables, views, and private synonyms. If the object is a private synonym, then Oracle locates the object for

which the synonym stands. This object could be in your own schema, another schema, or on another database. The object could also be another synonym, in which case Oracle locates the object for which this synonym stands.

2. If the object is in the namespace, then Oracle attempts to perform the statement on the object. In this example, Oracle attempts to add the row of data to departments. If the object is not of the correct type for the statement, then Oracle returns an error. In this example, departments must be a table, view, or a private synonym resolving to a table or view. If departments is a sequence, then Oracle returns an error.

3. If the object is not in any namespace searched in thus far, then Oracle searches the namespace containing public synonyms. If the object is in that namespace, then Oracle attempts to perform the statement on it. If the object is not of the correct type for the statement, then Oracle returns an error. In this example, if departments is a public synonym for a sequence, then Oracle returns an error.

If a public synonym has any dependent tables or user-defined types, then you cannot create an object with the same name as the synonym in the same schema as the dependent objects.

If a synonym does not have any dependent tables or user-defined types, then you can create an object with the same name in the same schema as the dependent objects. Oracle invalidates any dependent objects and attempts to revalidate them when they are next accessed.

32. Which two options are not true when you execute a COMMIT statement?

a) All locks created by DML statements are released in the session.
b) All SAVEPOINTS created are erased in the session.
c) Queries started before COMMIT in other sessions will show the current changes after COMMIT.
d) All undo information written from the DML statements is erased.

Answer: c, d

Explanation:

When COMMIT is executed, all locks are released, all savepoints are erased, and queries started before the COMMIT will constitute a read-consistent view using the undo information.

33. Which operator is used to add more joining conditions in a multiple-table query?

a) NOT
b) NOR
c) AND
d) Comma (,)

Answer: c

Explanation:

The operators OR and AND are used to add more joining conditions to the query. NOT is a negation operator, and a comma is used to separate column names and table names.

34. What is wrong with the following SQL?

SELECT department_id, MAX(COUNT(*))

FROM employees
GROUP BY department_id;

a) Aggregate functions cannot be nested.
b) The GROUP BY clause should not be included when using nested aggregate functions.
c) The department_id column in the SELECT clause should not be used when using nested aggregate functions.
d) The COUNT function cannot be nested.

Answer: c

Explanation:

Since you are finding the aggregate of the aggregate, you should not use nonaggregate columns in the SELECT clause.

35. **Which types of constraints can be created on a view?**

a) Check, NOT NULL
b) Primary key, foreign key, unique key
c) Check, NOT NULL, primary key, foreign key, unique key
d) No constraints can be created on a view.

Answer: b

Explanation:

You can create primary key, foreign key, and unique key constraints on a view. The constraints on views are not enforced by Oracle. To enforce a constraint, it must be defined on a table. Views can be created with the WITH CHECK OPTION and READ ONLY attributes during view creation

36. **Which two declarations define the maximum length of a CHAR datatype column in bytes?**

a) CHAR (20)
b) CHAR (20) BYTE
c) BYTE (20 CHAR)
d) CHAR BYTE (20)

Answer: a

Explanation:

The maximum lengths of CHAR and VARCHAR2 columns can be defined in characters or bytes. BYTE is the default.

37. **A view is created using the following code. Which of the following operations are permitted on the view?**

```
CREATE VIEW USA_STATES
AS SELECT * FROM STATE
WHERE CNT_CODE = 1
WITH READ ONLY;
```

a) SELECT
b) SELECT, UPDATE
c) SELECT, DELETE
d) SELECT, INSERT

Answer: a

Explanation:

When the view is created with the READ ONLY option, only reads are allowed from the view.

38. **You query the database with the following:**

```
SELECT PRODUCT_ID FROM PRODUCTS
WHERE PRODUCT_ID LIKE '%S\_J\_C' ESCAPE '\';
```

Choose the two PRODUCT_ID strings that will satisfy the query.

a) BTS_J_C
b) SJC
c) SKJKC
d) SK_J_C

Answer: a

Explanation:

The substitution character % can be substituted for zero or many characters. The substitution character _ does not have any effect in this query because an escape character precedes it, so it is treated as a literal.

39. **The EMPLOYEE table is defined as follows:**

```
EMP_NAME VARCHAR2(40)
HIRE_DATE DATE
SALARY NUMBER (14,2)
```

Which query is most appropriate to use if you need to find the employees who were hired before January 1, 1998 and have a salary greater than 5,000 or less than 1,000?

a) SELECT emp_name FROM employee
   WHERE hire_date > TO_DATE('01011998','MMDDYYYY')
   AND SALARY < 1000 OR > 5000;
b) SELECT emp_name FROM employee

```
WHERE hire_date < TO_DATE('01011998','MMDDYYYY')
AND SALARY < 1000 OR SALARY > 5000;
```

c) ```
SELECT emp_name FROM employee
WHERE hire_date < TO_DATE('01011998','MMDDYYYY')
AND (SALARY < 1000 OR SALARY > 5000);
```

d) ```
SELECT emp_name FROM employee
WHERE hire_date < TO_DATE('01011998','MMDDYYYY')
AND SALARY BETWEEN 1000 AND 5000;
```

Answer: c

Explanation:

You have two main conditions in the question: one on the hire date and the other on the salary. So, you should use an AND operator. In the second part, you have two options: the salary can be either more than 5,000 or less than 1,000, so the second part should be enclosed in parentheses and should use an OR operator. Option b is similar to option C except for the parentheses, but the difference changes the meaning completely. Option b would select the employees who were hired before January 1, 1998 or have a salary greater than 5,000 or less than 1,000.

40. **What happens when you issue the following command? (Choose one that apply.)**

TRUNCATE TABLE SCOTT.EMPLOYEE;

a) All the rows in the table EMPLOYEE owned by SCOTT are removed.
b) If foreign key constraints are defined to this table using the ON DELETE CASCADE clause, the rows from the child tables are also removed.
c) The indexes on the table are dropped.
d) You cannot truncate a table if triggers are defined on the table.

Answer: a

Explanation:

The TRUNCATE command is used to remove all the rows from a table or cluster. By default, this command releases all the storage space used by the table and resets the table's high-water mark to zero. No indexes, constraints, or triggers on the table are dropped or disabled. If there are valid foreign key constraints defined to this table, you must disable all of them before truncating the table.

41. **Which statements will drop the primary key defined on table EMP? The primary key name is PK_EMP.**

a) ALTER TABLE EMP DROP PRIMARY KEY;
b) DROP CONSTRAINT PK_EMP;
c) ALTER CONSTRAINT PK_EMP DROP CASCADE;
d) DROP CONSTRAINT PK_EMP ON EMP;

Answer: a

Explanation:

Since there can be only one primary key per table, the syntax in option a works.

42. If a table is created without specifying a schema, in which schema will it be? (Choose the best answer.)

    a) It will be an orphaned table, without a schema.
    b) The creation will fail.
    c) It will be in the SYS schema.
    d) It will be in the schema of the user creating it.

    Answer: d

    Explanation:

    Option d is correct because the schema will default to the current user.

    Option a is wrong because all tables must be in a schema.
    Option b is wrong because the creation will succeed.
    Option c is wrong because the SYS schema is not a default schema.

43. Several object types share the same namespace and therefore cannot have the same name in the same schema. Which of the following object types is not in the same namespace as the others? (Choose the best answer.)

    a) Index
    b) PL/SQL stored procedure
    c) Synonym
    d) Table

    Answer: a

    Explanation:

    Indexes have their own namespace.

    Option b, PL/SQL stored procedures exist in the same namespace.
    Option c Synonym exist in the same namespace.
    Option d. tables and views exist in the same namespace.

44. Which of these statements will fail because the table name is not legal? (Choose one answer.)

a) create table "SELECT" (col1 date);
b) create table "lowercase" (col1 date);
c) create table number1 (col1 date);
d) create table 1number(col1 date);

Answer: d

Explanation:

Option d violates the rule that a table name must begin with a letter. This rule can be bypassed by using double quotes.

Option a, b, and c. These are wrong because all will succeed (though A and B are not exactly sensible).

Illustration:

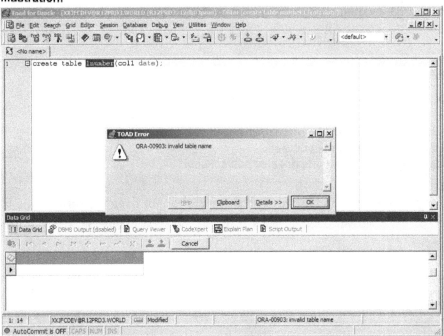

45. What are distinguishing characteristics of heap tables? (Choose one answer.)

a) A heap table can store variable-length rows.
b) More than one table can store rows in a single heap.
c) Tables in a heap do not have a primary key.
d) Heap tables cannot be indexed.

Answer: a

Explanation:

Option a heap is a table of variable-length rows in random order.

Option b is wrong because a heap table can only be one table.
Option d is wrong because a heap table can (and usually will) have indexes and a primary key.

46. **Which of the following data types is not variable length? (Choose all correct answers.)**

   a) BLOB
   b) CHAR
   c) LONG
   d) NUMBER

   Answer: b

   Explanation:

   Option b CHAR columns are fixed length.

   Option a, c and d. All these are variable-length data types.

47. **Study these statements:**

   ```
   create table tab1 (c1 number(1), c2 date);
   alter session set nls_date_format='dd-mm-yy';
   insert into tab1 values (1.1,'31-01-07');
   ```

   Will the insert succeed? (Choose the best answer.)

   a) The insert will fail because the 1.1 is too long.
   b) The insert will fail because the '31-01-07' is a string, not a date.
   c) The insert will fail for both reasons A and B.
   d) The insert will succeed.

   Answer: d

   Explanation:

   Option d. The number will be rounded to one digit, and the string will cast as a date.

   Option a. b and c. Automatic rounding and typecasting will correct the "errors," though ideally they would not occur.

48. **Which of the following is not supported by Oracle as an internal data type? (Choose the best answer.)**

   a) CHAR
   b) FLOAT
   c) INTEGER

d) STRING

Answer: d

Explanation:

Option d. STRING is not an internal data type.

Option a, b and c. CHAR, FLOAT, and INTEGER are all internal data types, though not as widely used as some others.

49. **Consider this statement:**

create table t1 as select * from regions where 1=2;

What will be the result? (Choose the best answer.)

a) There will be an error because of the impossible condition.
b) No table will be created because the condition returns FALSE.
c) The table T1 will be created but no rows inserted because the condition returns FALSE.
d) The table T1 will be created and every row in REGIONS inserted because the condition returns a NULL as a row filter.

Answer: c

Explanation:

Option c. The condition applies only to the rows selected for insert, not to the table creation.

Option a is wrong because the statement is syntactically correct.
Option b is wrong because the condition does not apply to the DDL, only to the DML.
Option d is wrong because the condition will exclude all rows from selection.

Illustration:

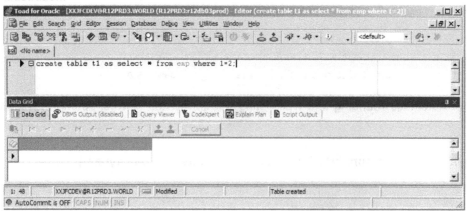

50. **When a table is created with a statement such as the following:**

create table newtab as select * from tab;

Will there be any constraints on the new table? (Choose the best answer.)

a) The new table will have no constraints, because constraints are not copied when creating tables with a subquery.
b) All the constraints on TAB will be copied to NEWTAB.
c) Primary key and unique constraints will be copied, but not check and notnull constraints.
d) Check and not-null constraints will be copied, but not unique or primary keys.

Answer: d

Explanation:

Option d. Check and not-null constraints are not dependent on any structures other than the table to which they apply and so can safely be copied to a new table.

Option a is wrong because not-null and check constraints will be applied to the new table.

Option b and c are wrong because these constraints need other objects (indexes or a parent table) and so are not copied.

51. **Which types of constraint require an index? (Choose all that apply.)**

a) CHECK
b) NOT NULL
c) FOREIGN KEY
d) UNIQUE

Answer: d

Explanation:

Option d. Unique and primary key constraints are enforced with indexes.

Option a, b and c. Check and not-null constraints do not rely on indexes.

52. **A transaction consists of two statements. The first succeeds, but the second (which updates several rows) fails partway through because of a constraint violation. What will happen? (Choose the best answer.)**

a) The whole transaction will be rolled back.
b) The second statement will be rolled back completely, and the first will be committed.
c) The second statement will be rolled back completely, and the first will remain uncommitted.
d) Only the one update that caused the violation will be rolled back, everything else will be committed.

Answer: c

Explanation:

Option c. A constraint violation will force a rollback of the current statement but nothing else.

Option a is wrong because all statements that have succeeded remain intact.

Option b and d are wrong because there is no commit of anything until it is specifically requested.

53. **Which of the following statements is correct about indexes? (Choose the best answer.)**

    a) An index can be based on multiple columns of a table, but the columns must be of the same datatype.
    b) An index can be based on multiple columns of a table, but the columns must be adjacent and specified in the order that they are defined in the table.
    c) An index cannot have the same name as a table, unless the index and the table are in separate schemas.
    d) None of the above statements is correct

    Answer: d

    Explanation:

    Option d. All the statements are wrong.

    Option a is wrong because compound indexes need not be on columns of the same datatype.

    Option b is wrong because the columns in a compound index need not be physically adjacent.

    Option c is wrong because indexes and tables do not share the same namespace.

54. **Which of the following options can be applied to B*Tree indexes, but not to bitmap indexes? (Choose all correct answers.)**

    a) Compression
    b) Descending order
    c) Function-based key expressions
    d) Use of compound keys

    Answer: a

    Explanation:

    Option a. Compression can be applied to B*Tree indexes.

    Option b, c and d. Descending, function-based, and compound indexes can be either B*Tree or bitmap.

55. Data in temporary tables has restricted visibility. If a user logs on as HR and inserts rows into a temporary table, to whom will the rows be visible?

a) To no session other than the one that did the insert
b) To all sessions connected as HR
c) To all sessions, until the session that inserted them terminates
d) To all sessions, until the session that inserted them commits the transaction

Answer: a

Explanation:

Option a. Rows in a temporary table are visible only the inserting session.

Option b, c and d. All these incorrectly describe the scope of visibility of rows in a temporary table.

56. Where does the data in a temporary table get written to disk? (Choose the best answer.)

a) It is never written to disk
b) To the user's temporary tablespace
c) To the temporary tablespace of the user in whose schema the table resides
d) To a disk local to the session's user process

Answer: b

Explanation:

Option b. If a temporary table cannot fit in a session's PGA, it will be written to the session's temporary tablespace.

Option a is wrong because temporary tables can be written out to temporary segments.

Option c is wrong because the location of the temporary segment is session specific, not table specific.

Option d is wrong because it is the session server process that writes the data, not the user process.

57. Which of these is a defining characteristic of a complex view, rather than a simple view? (Choose one correct answer.)

a) Restricting the projection by selecting only some of the table's columns
b) Naming the view's columns with column aliases
c) Restricting the selection of rows with a WHERE clause
d) Performing an aggregation

Answer: d

Explanation:

Option d. Aggregations and joins make a view complex and make DML impossible.

Option a, b and c. Selection and projection or renaming columns does not make the view complex.

58. **Consider these three statements:**

create view v1 as select department_id,department_name,last_name from
departments join employees using (department_id);
select department_name,last_name from v1 where department_id=20;
select d.department_name,e.last_name from departments d, employees e
where d.department_id=e.department_id and
d.department_id=20;

The first query will be quicker than the second because (choose the best answer):

a) The view has already done the work of joining the tables.
b) The view uses ISO standard join syntax, which is faster than the Oracle join syntax used in the second query.
c) The view is precompiled, so the first query requires less dynamic compilation than the second query.
d) There is no reason for the first query to be quicker.

Answer: d

Explanation:

Option d. Sad but true. Views will not help performance, unless they include tuning hints.

Option a is wrong because a view is only a SELECT statement; it doesn't prerun the query.

Option b is wrong because the Oracle optimizer will sort out any differences in syntax.

Option c is wrong because, although views are precompiled, this doesn't affect the speed of compiling a user's statement.

59. **Study this view creation statement:**

create view dept30 as
select department_id,employee_id,last_name from employees
where department_id=30 with check option;

What might make the following statement fail? (Choose the best answer.)

update dept30 set department_id=10 where employee_id=114;

a) Unless specified otherwise, views will be created as WITH READ ONLY.
b) The view is too complex to allow DML operations.
c) The WITH CHECK OPTION will reject any statement that changes the DEPARTMENT_ID.
d) The statement will succeed.

Answer: c

Explanation:

Option c. The WITH CHECK OPTION will prevent DML that would cause a row to disappear from the view.

Option a is wrong because views are by default created read/write.

Option b is wrong because the view is a simple view.

Option d is wrong because the statement cannot succeed because the check option will reject it.

60. **There is a simple view SCOTT.DEPT_VIEW on the table SCOTT.DEPT. This insert fails with an error:**

    ```
    SQL> insert into dept_view values('SUPPORT','OXFORD');
    insert into dept_view values('SUPPORT','OXFORD')
    *
    ERROR at line 1:
    ORA-01400: cannot insert NULL into ("SCOTT"."DEPT"."DEPTNO")
    ```

    What might be the problem? (Choose the best answer.)

    a) The INSERT violates a constraint on the detail table.
    b) The INSERT violates a constraint on the view.
    c) The view was created as WITH READ ONLY.
    d) The view was created as WITH CHECK OPTION.

    Answer: a

    Explanation:

    Option a. There is a NOT NULL or PRIMARY KEY constraint on DEPT.DEPTNO.

    Option B is wrong because constraints are enforced on detail tables, not on views.

    Option c and d are wrong because the error message would be different.

61. **What are distinguishing characteristics of a public synonym rather than a private synonym? (Choose two correct answers.)**

    a) Public synonyms are always visible to all users.
    b) Public synonyms can be accessed by name without a schema name qualifier.
    c) Public synonyms can be selected from without needing any permissions.
    d) Public synonyms can have the same names as tables or views.

    Answer: b and d

Explanation:

Option b and d. Public synonyms are not schema objects and so can only be addressed directly. They can have the same names as schema objects.

Option a and c. These are wrong because users must be granted privileges on a public synonym before they can see it or select from it.

62. **Consider these three statements:**

    create synonym s1 for employees;
    create public synonym s1 for departments;
    select * from s1;

    Which of the following statements is correct? (Choose the best answer.)

    a) The second statement will fail because an object S1 already exists.
    b) The third statement will show the contents of EMPLOYEES.
    c) The third statement will show the contents of DEPARTMENTS.
    d) The third statement will show the contents of the table S1, if such a table exists in the current schema.

    Answer: b

    Explanation:

    Option b. The order of priority is to search the schema namespace before the public namespace, so it will be the private synonym (to EMPLOYEES) that will be found.

    Option a is wrong because a synonym can exist in both the public namespace and the schema namespace.

    Option c is wrong because the order of priority will find the private synonym first.

    Option d is wrong because it would not be possible to have a table and a private synonym in the same schema with the same name.

63. **A view and a synonym are created as follows:**

    create view dept_v as select * from dept;
    create synonym dept_s for dept_v;

    Subsequently the table DEPT is dropped. What will happen if you query the synonym DEPT_S ? (Choose the best answer.)

    a) There will not be an error because the synonym addresses the view, which still exists, but there will be no rows returned.
    b) There will not be an error if you first recompile the view with the command ALTER VIEW DEPT_V COMPILE FORCE;.

c) There will be an error because the synonym will be invalid.
d) There will be an error because the view will be invalid.

Answer: d

Explanation:

Option d. The synonym will be fine, but the view will be invalid. Oracle will attempt to recompile the view, but this will fail.

Option a is wrong because the view will be invalid.

Option b is wrong because the FORCE keyword can only be applied when creating a view (and it would still be invalid, even so).

Option c is wrong because the synonym will be fine.

64. **A sequence is created as follows:**

create sequence seq1 maxvalue 50;

If the current value is already 50, when you attempt to select SEQ1.NEXTVAL

What will happen? (Choose the best answer.)

a) The sequence will cycle and issue 0.
b) The sequence will cycle and issue 1.
c) The sequence will reissue 50.
d) There will be an error.

Answer: d

Explanation:

Option d. The default is NOCYCLE, and the sequence cannot advance further.

Option a and b are wrong because CYCLE is disabled by default. If it were enabled, the next number issued would be 1 (not zero) because 1 is the default for START WITH.

Option c is wrong because under no circumstances will a sequence issue repeating values.

65. **You create a sequence as follows:**

create sequence seq1 start with 1;

After selecting from it a few times, you want to reinitialize it to reissue the numbers already generated. How can you do this? (Choose the best answer.)

a) You must drop and re-create the sequence.
b) You can't. Under no circumstances can numbers from a sequence be reissued once they have been used.

c) Use the command ALTER SEQUENCE SEQ1 START WITH 1; to reset the next value to 1.

d) Use the command ALTER SEQUENCE SEQ1 CYCLE; to reset the sequence to its starting value.

Answer: a

Explanation:

Option a. It is not possible to change the next value of a sequence, so you must recreate it.

Option b is wrong because, while a NOCYCLE sequence can never reissue numbers, there is no reason why a new sequence (with the same name) cannot do so.

Option c is wrong because START WITH can only be specified at creation time.

Option d is wrong because this will not force an instant cycle, it will only affect what happens when the sequence reaches its MAXVALUE or MINVALUE.

66. **Which of the following commands cannot be rolled back? (Choose all correct answers.)**

a) COMMIT
b) DELETE
c) INSERT
d) MERGE

Answer: a

Explanation:

Option a. COMMIT terminates a transaction, which can then never be rolled back.

Option b, c and d are the DML commands: they can all be rolled back.

67. **If an UPDATE or DELETE command has a WHERE clause that gives it a scope of several rows, what will happen if there is an error part way through execution? The command is one of several in a multi-statement transaction. (Choose the best answer.)**

a) The command will skip the row that caused the error and continue.
b) The command will stop at the error, and the rows that have been updated or deleted will remain updated or deleted.
c) Whatever work the command had done before hitting the error will be rolled back, but work done already by the transaction will remain.
d) The whole transaction will be rolled back.

Answer: c

Explanation:

Option c. This is the expected behavior: the statement is rolled back, and the rest of the transaction remains uncommitted.

Option a is wrong because, while this behavior is in fact configurable, it is not enabled by default.

Option b is wrong because, while this is in fact possible in the event of space errors, it is not enabled by default.

Option d is wrong because only the one statement will be rolled back, not the whole transaction.

68. **Study the result of this SELECT statement:**

```
SQL> select * from t1;
C1 C2 C3 C4
---------- ---------- ---------- ----------
 1  2  3  4
 5  6  7  8
```

If you issue this statement:

insert into t1 (c1,c2) values(select c1,c2 from t1);

Why will it fail? (Choose the best answer.)

a) Because values are not provided for all the table's columns: there should be NULLs for C3 and C4.
b) Because the subquery returns multiple rows: it requires a WHERE clause to restrict the number of rows returned to one.
c) Because the subquery is not scalar: it should use MAX or MIN to generate scalar values.
d) Because the VALUES keyword is not used with a subquery.
e) It will succeed, inserting two rows with NULLs for C3 and C4.

Answer: d

Explanation:

Option d. The syntax is wrong: use either the VALUES keyword or a subquery, but not both. Remove the VALUES keyword, and it will run. C3 and C4 would be populated with NULLs.

Option a is wrong because there is no need to provide values for columns not listed.

Option b and c are wrong because an INSERT can insert a set of rows, so there is no need to restrict the number with a WHERE clause or by using MAX or MIN to return only one row.

Option e is wrong because the statement is not syntactically correct.

69. **You want to insert a row and then update it. What sequence of steps should you follow? (Choose the best answer.)**

a) INSERT, UPDATE, COMMIT
b) INSERT, COMMIT, UPDATE, COMMIT
c) INSERT, SELECT FOR UPDATE, UPDATE, COMMIT
d) INSERT, COMMIT, SELECT FOR UPDATE, UPDATE, COMMIT

Answer: a

Explanation:

Option a is the simplest (and therefore the best) way.

Option b, c and d will work, but they are all needlessly complicated: no programmer should use unnecessary statements.

70. **Which of these commands will remove every row in a table? (Choose one or more correct answers.)**

    a) A DELETE command with no WHERE clause
    b) A DROP TABLE command
    c) A TRUNCATE command
    d) An UPDATE command, setting every column to NULL and with no WHERE clause

    Answer: a, c

    Explanation:

    Option a and c. The TRUNCATE will be faster, but the DELETE will get there too.

    Option b is wrong because this will remove the table as well as the rows within it.
    Option d is wrong because the rows will still be there—even though they are populated with NULLs.

71. **User JOHN updates some rows and asks user ROOPESH to log in and check the changes before he commits them. Which of the following statements is true? (Choose the best answer.)**

    a) ROOPESH can see the changes but cannot alter them because JOHN will have locked the rows.
    b) ROOPESH will not be able to see the changes.
    c) JOHN must commit the changes so that ROOPESH can see them and, if necessary, roll them back.
    d) JOHN must commit the changes so that ROOPESH can see them, but only JOHN can roll them back.

    Answer: a

    Explanation:

    Option b. The principle of isolation means that only JOHN can see his uncommitted transaction.

    Option a is wrong because transaction isolation means that no other session will be able to see the changes.

    Option c and d are wrong because a committed transaction can never be rolled back.

72. **When a COMMIT is issued, what will happen?**

a) All the change vectors that make up the transaction are written to disk.
b) DBWn writes the change blocks to disk.
c) LGWR writes the log buffer to disk.
d) The undo data is deleted, so that the changes can no longer be rolled back.

Answer: c

Explanation:

Option c. A COMMIT is implemented by placing a COMMIT record in the log buffer, and LGWR flushing the log buffer to disk.

Option a is wrong because many of the change vectors (perhaps all of them) will be on disk already.

Option b is wrong because DBWn does not participate in commit processing.

Option d is wrong because the undo data may well persist for some time; a COMMIT is not relevant to this.

73. **What types of segment is not protected by redo?**

a) Index segments
b) Table segments
c) Temporary segments
d) Undo segments

Answer: c

Explanation:

Option c. Changes to temporary segments do not generate redo.

Option a, b and d changes to any of these will generate redo.

74. **Which of these commands will terminate a transaction? (Choose all correct answers.)**

a) CREATE
b) GRANT
c) SAVEPOINT
d) SET AUTOCOMMIT ON

Answer: a and b

Explanation:

Option a and b. Both DDL and access control commands include a COMMIT.

Option c is wrong because a SAVEPOINT is only a marker within a transaction.

Option d is wrong because this is a SQL*Plus command that acts locally on the user process; it has no effect on an active transaction.

75. **What type of PL/SQL objects cannot be packaged? (Choose the best answer.)**

    a) Functions
    b) Procedures
    c) Triggers
    d) All PL/SQL objects can be packaged, except anonymous blocks

    Answer: c

    Explanation:

    Option c triggers cannot be packaged.

    Option a and b are wrong because functions and procedures can be packaged.

    Option d is wrong because neither anonymous blocks nor triggers can be packaged.

76. **If several sessions request an exclusive lock on the same row, what will happen? (Choose the best answer.)**

    a) The first session will get the lock; after it releases the lock there is a random selection of the next session to get the lock.
    b) The first session will get an exclusive lock, and the other sessions will get shared locks.
    c) The sessions will be given an exclusive lock in the sequence in which they requested it.
    d) Oracle will detect the conflict and roll back the statements that would otherwise hang.

    Answer: c

    Explanation:

    Option c correctly describes the operation of the enqueue mechanism.

    Option a is wrong because locks are granted sequentially, not randomly.

    Option b is wrong because the shared locks apply to the object; row locks must be exclusive.

    Option d is wrong because this is more like a description of how deadlocks are managed.

77. **When a DML statement executes, what happens? (Choose the best answer.)**

    a) Both the data and the undo blocks on disk are updated, and the changes are written out to the redo stream.
    b) The old version of the data is written to an undo segment, and the new version is written to the data segments and the redo log buffer.
    c) Both data and undo blocks are updated in the database buffer cache, and the updates also go to the log buffer.

d) The redo log buffer is updated with information needed to redo the transaction, and the undo blocks are updated with information needed to reverse the transaction.

Answer: c

Explanation:

Option c. All DML occurs in the database buffer cache, and changes to both data block and undo blocks are protected by redo.

Option a is wrong because writing to disk is independent of executing the statement.

Option b and d are incomplete: redo protects changes to both data blocks and undo blocks.

78. **Your undo tablespace consists of one datafile on one disk, and transactions are failing for lack of undo space. The disk is full. You have enabled retention guarantee. Any of the following options could solve the problem, but which would cause down time for your users? (Choose the best answer.)**

    a) Create another, larger, undo tablespace and use "alter system set undo_ tablespace= . . ." to switch to it.
    b) Move the datafile to a disk with more space, and use "alter database resize datafile . . ." to make it bigger.
    c) Reduce the undo_retention setting with "alter system set undo_retention= . . . ."
    d) Disable retention guarantee with "alter tablespace . . . retention guarantee."

    Answer: b

    Explanation:

    Option b. This is the option that would require downtime, because the datafile would have to taken offline during the move and you cannot take it offline while the database is open.

    Option a, c and d are wrong because they are all operations that can be carried out during normal running without end users being aware.

79. **Examine this query and result set:**

```
SQL> select BEGIN_TIME,END_TIME,UNDOBLKS,MAXQUERYLEN from V$UNDOSTAT;

BEGIN_TIME          END_TIME            UNDOBLKS    MAXQUERYLEN
----------------    ------------------  ----------  -----------
02-01-08:11:35:55   02-01-08:11:41:33   14435 29
02-01-08:11:25:55   02-01-08:11:35:55   120248 296
02-01-08:11:15:55   02-01-08:11:25:55   137497 37
02-01-08:11:05:55   02-01-08:11:15:55   102760 1534
02-01-08:10:55:55   02-01-08:11:05:55   237014 540
02-01-08:10:45:55   02-01-08:10:55:55   156223 1740
02-01-08:10:35:55   02-01-08:10:45:55   145275 420
02-01-08:10:25:55   02-01-08:10:35:55   99074 120
```

The blocksize of the undo tablespace is 4KB. Which of the following would be the optimal size for the undo tablespace? (Choose the best answer.)

a) 1GB
b) 2GB
c) 3GB
d) 4GB

Answer: c

Explanation:

Option c. To calculate, take the largest figure for UNDBLKS, which is for a ten minute period. Divide by 600 to get the rate of undo generation in blocks per second, and multiply by the block size to get the figure in bytes. Multiply by the largest figure for MAXQUERYLEN, to find the space needed if the highest rate of undo generation coincided with the longest query, and divide by a billion to get the answer in gigabytes: 237014 / 600 * 4192 * 1740 = 2.9 (approximately)

Option a, b and d are wrong. The following algorithm should be followed when sizing an undo tablespace: Calculate the rate at which undo is being generated at your peak workload, and multiply by the length of your longest query.

80. Which query will create a projection of the DEPARTMENT_NAME and LOCATION_ID columns from the DEPARTMENTS table? (Choose the best answer.)

a) SELECT DISTINCT DEPARTMENT_NAME, LOCATION_ID FROM DEPARTMENTS;
b) SELECT DEPARTMENT_NAME, LOCATION_ID FROM DEPARTMENTS;
c) SELECT DEPT_NAME, LOC_ID FROM DEPT;
d) SELECT DEPARTMENT_NAME AS "LOCATION_ID" FROM DEPARTMENTS;

Answer: b

Explanation:

Option b. A projection is an intentional restriction of the columns returned from a table.

Option a is eliminated since the question has nothing to do with duplicates, distinctiveness, or uniqueness of data.

Option c incorrectly selects nonexistent columns called DEPT_NAME and LOC_ID from a nonexistent table called DEPT.

Option d returns just one of the requested columns: DEPARTMENT_NAME. Instead of additionally projecting the LOCATION_ID column from the DEPARTMENTS table, it attempts to alias the DEPARTMENT_NAME column as LOCATION_ID.

81. After describing the EMPLOYEES table, you discover that the SALARY column has a data type of NUMBER(8,2). Which SALARY value(s) will not be permitted in this column? (Choose the best answer.)

a) SALARY=12345678
b) SALARY=123456.78
c) SALARY=1234567.8

d) SALARY=123456

Answer: a

Explanation:

Option a. Columns with the NUMBER(8,2) data type can store at most eight digits, of which at most two of those digits are to the right of the decimal point. Although A is the correct answers, note that since the question is phrased in the negative, these values are not allowed to be stored in such a column. A is not allowed because they contain eight and seven whole number digits respectively, but the data type is constrained to store six whole number digits and two fractional digits.

Option b, c and d can legitimately be stored in this data type and, therefore, are the incorrect answers to this question. D shows that numbers with no fractional part are legitimate values for this column, as long as the number of digits in the whole number portion does not exceed six digits.

82. After describing the JOB_HISTORY table, you discover that the START_DATE and END_DATE columns have a data type of DATE. Consider the expression "END_DATE – START_DATE". Choose two correct statements regarding this expression.

    a) A value of DATE data type is returned.
    b) A value of type NUMBER is returned.
    c) A value of type VARCHAR2 is returned.
    d) The expression is invalid, since arithmetic cannot be performed on columns with DATE data types.

    Answer: b

    Explanation:

    Option b. The result of arithmetic between two date values represents a certain number of days.

    Option a, c and d are incorrect. It is a common mistake to expect the result of arithmetic between two date values to be a date as well, so A may seem plausible, but it is false.

83. Which statement reports on unique JOB_ID values from the EMPLOYEES table? (Choose the best answer.)

    a) SELECT JOB_ID FROM EMPLOYEES;
    b) SELECT UNIQUE JOB_ID FROM EMPLOYEES;
    c) SELECT DISTINCT JOB_ID, EMPLOYEE_ID FROM EMPLOYEES;
    d) SELECT DISTINCT JOB_ID FROM EMPLOYEES;

    Answer: d

    Explanation:

    Option d. Unique JOB_ID values are projected from the EMPLOYEES table by applying the DISTINCT keyword to just the JOB_ID column.

Option a, b and c are eliminated, since A returns an unrestricted list of JOB_ID values including duplicates; B makes use of the UNIQUE keyword in the incorrect context; and C selects the distinct combination of JOB_ID and EMPLOYEE_ID values. This has the effect of returning all the rows from the EMPLOYEES table, since the EMPLOYEE_ID column contains unique values for each employee record. Additionally, C returns two columns, which is not what was originally requested.

84. Choose the two illegal statements. The two correct statements produce identical results. The two illegal statements will cause an error to be raised:

a) SELECT DEPARTMENT_ID|| ' represents the '|| DEPARTMENT_NAME||' Department' as "Department Info" FROM DEPARTMENTS;
b) SELECT DEPARTMENT_ID|| ' represents the || DEPARTMENT_NAME||' Department' as "Department Info" FROM DEPARTMENTS;
c) select department_id|| ' represents the '||department_name|| ' Department' "Department Info" from departments;
d) SELECT DEPARTMENT_ID represents the DEPARTMENT_NAME Department as "Department Info" FROM DEPARTMENTS;

Answer: b and d

Explanation:

Option b and d represent the two illegal statements that will return syntax errors if they are executed. This is a tricky question because it asks for the illegal statements and not the legal statements. B is illegal because it is missing a single quote enclosing the character literal "represents the". D is illegal because it does not make use of single quotes to enclose its character literals.

Option a and c are the legal statements and, therefore, in the context of the question, are the incorrect answers. A and C appear to be different, since the SQL statements differ in case and A uses the alias keyword AS, whereas C just leaves a space between the expression and the alias. Yet both A and C produce identical results.

85. Which two clauses of the SELECT statement facilitate selection and projection? (Choose the best answer.)

a) SELECT, FROM
b) ORDER BY, WHERE
c) SELECT, WHERE
d) SELECT, ORDER BY

Answer: c

Explanation:

Option c. The SELECT clause facilitates projection by specifying the list of columns to be projected from a table, while the WHERE clause facilitates selection by limiting the rows retrieved based on its conditions.

Option a, b and d are incorrect because the FROM clause specifies the source of the rows being projected and the ORDER BY clause is used for sorting the selected rows.

86. Choose the WHERE clause that extracts the DEPARTMENT_NAME values containing the character literal "er" from the DEPARTMENTS table. The SELECT and FROM clauses are SELECT DEPARTMENT_NAME FROM DEPARTMENTS: (Choose the best answer.)

    a) WHERE DEPARTMENT_NAME IN ('%e%r');
    b) WHERE DEPARTMENT_NAME LIKE '%er%';
    c) WHERE DEPARTMENT_NAME BETWEEN 'e' AND 'r';
    d) WHERE DEPARTMENT_NAME CONTAINS 'e%r'

    Answer: b

    Explanation:

    Option b. The LIKE operator tests the DEPARTMENT_NAME column of each row for values that contain the characters "er". The percentage symbols before and after the character literal indicate that any characters enclosing the "er" literal are permissible.

    Option a and c are syntactically correct. A uses the IN operator, which is used to test set membership. C tests whether the alphabetic value of the DEPARTMENT_NAME column is between the letter "e" and the letter "r." Finally, option d uses the word "contains," which cannot be used in this context.

87. Which of the following conditions are equivalent to each other? (Choose all correct answers.)

    a) WHERE SALARY <=5000 AND SALARY >=2000
    b) WHERE SALARY IN (2000,3000,4000,5000)
    c) WHERE SALARY > 2000 AND SALARY < 5000
    d) WHERE SALARY >=2000 AND <=5000

    Answer: a

    Explanation:

    Option a. Each of these conditions tests for SALARY values in the range of $2000 to $5000.

    Option b, c and d are incorrect. B excludes values like $2500 from its set. C excludes the boundary values of $2000 and $5000, and D is illegal since it is missing the SALARY column name reference after the AND operator.

88. Choose one false statement about the ORDER BY clause. (Choose the best answer.)

    a) When using the ORDER BY clause, it always appears as the last clause in a SELECT statement.
    b) The ORDER BY clause may appear in a SELECT statement that does not contain a WHERE clause.
    c) The ORDER BY clause specifies one or more terms by which the retrieved rows are sorted. These terms can only be column names.
    d) Positional sorting is accomplished by specifying the numeric position of a column as it appears in the SELECT list, in the ORDER BY clause.

    Answer: c

Explanation:

Option c. The terms specified in an ORDER BY clause can include column names, positional sorting, numeric values, and expressions.

Option a, b and d are true.

89. When using ampersand substitution variables in the following query, how many times will you be prompted to input a value for the variable called JOB the first time this query is executed?

```
SELECT FIRST_NAME, '&JOB'
FROM EMPLOYEES
WHERE JOB_ID LIKE '%'||&JOB||'%'
AND '&&JOB' BETWEEN 'A' AND 'Z';
```

(Choose the best answer.)

a) 0
b) 1
c) 2
d) 3

Answer: d

Explanation:

Option d. The first time this statement is executed, two single ampersand substitution variables are encountered before the third double ampersand substitution variable. If the first reference on line one of the query contained a double ampersand substitution, you would only be prompted to input a value once.

Option a, b and c are incorrect, since you are prompted three times to input a value for the JOB substitution variable. In subsequent executions of this statement in the same session, you will not be prompted to input a value for this variable.

90. Which statements regarding single-row functions are true? (Choose all that apply.)

a) They may return more than one value.
b) They execute once for each row processed.
c) They may have zero or more input parameters.
d) They must have at least one mandatory parameter.

Answer: b, c

Explanation:

Option b and c. Single-row functions execute once for every record selected in a dataset and may either take no input parameters, like SYSDATE, or many input parameters.

Option a and d are incorrect because a function by definition returns only one result and there are many functions with no parameters.

91. What value is returned after executing the following statement: **SELECT SUBSTR('How_long_is_a_piece_of_string?', 5, 4) FROM DUAL;** (Choose the best answer.)

a) long
b) _long
c) ring?
d) None of the above

Answer: a

Explanation:

Option a. The SUBSTR function extracts a four-character substring from the given input string starting with and including the fifth character. The characters at positions 1 to 4 are "How_". Starting with the character at position 5, the next four characters form the word "long".

Option b, c and d are incorrect because B is a five-character substring beginning at position 4, while "ring?", which is also five characters long, starts five characters from the end of the given string.

92. What value is returned after executing the following statement:

```
SELECT INSTR('How_long_is_a_piece_of_string?','_', 5, 3)
FROM DUAL;
```

(Choose the best answer.)

a) 4
b) 14
c) 12
d) None of the above

Answer: b

Explanation:

Option b. The INSTR function returns the position that the nth occurrence of the search string may be found after starting the search from a given start position. The search string is the underscore character, and the third occurrence of this character starting from position 5 in the source string occurs at position 14.

Option a, c and d are incorrect, since position 4 is the first occurrence of the search string and position 12 is the third occurrence if the search began at position 1.

93. What value is returned after executing the following statement:

```
SELECT MOD(14, 3) FROM DUAL;
```

(Choose the best answer.)

a) 3
b) 42
c) 2
d) None of the above

Answer: c

Explanation:

Option c. When 14 is divided by 3, the answer is 4 with remainder 2.

Option a, b and d are incorrect.

94. **What value is returned after executing the following statement? Take note that 01-JAN-2009 occurred on a Thursday.**

```
SELECT NEXT_DAY('01-JAN-2009', 'wed') FROM DUAL;
```

(Choose the best answer.)

a) 07-JAN-2009
b) 31-JAN-2009
c) Wednesday
d) None of the above

Answer: a

Explanation:

Option a. Since the first of January 2009 falls on a Thursday, the date of the following Wednesday is six days later.

Option b, c and d are incorrect. B returns the last day of the month in which the given date falls, and C returns a character string instead of a date.

95. **Assuming SYSDATE=30-DEC-2007, what value is returned after executing the following statement:**

```
SELECT TRUNC(SYSDATE, 'YEAR') FROM DUAL;
```

(Choose the best answer.)

a) 31-DEC-2007
b) 01-JAN-2008
c) 01-JAN-2007
d) None of the above

Answer: c

Explanation:

Option c. The date TRUNC function does not perform rounding, and since the degree of truncation is YEAR, the day and month components of the given date are ignored and the first day of the year it belongs to is returned.

Option a, b and d are incorrect. A returns the last day in the month in which the given date occurs, and B returns a result achieved by rounding instead of truncation.

96. **Choose any incorrect statements regarding conversion functions. (Choose all that apply.)**

    a) TO_CHAR may convert date items to character items.
    b) TO_DATE may convert character items to date items.
    c) TO_CHAR may convert numbers to character items.
    d) TO_DATE may convert date items to character items.

    Answer: d

    Explanation:

    Option d. Dates are only converted into character strings using TO_CHAR, not the TO_DATE function.

    Option a, b and c are correct statements.

97. **If SYSDATE returns 12-JUL-2009, what is returned by the following statement?**

    ```
    SELECT TO_CHAR(SYSDATE, 'fmDDth MONTH') FROM DUAL;
    ```

    (Choose the best answer.)

    a) 12TH JULY
    b) 12th July
    c) TWELFTH JULY
    d) None of the above

    Answer: a

    Explanation:

    Option a. The DD component returns the day of the month in uppercase. Since it is a number, it does not matter, unless the 'th' mask is applied, in which case that component is specified in uppercase. MONTH returns the month spelled out in uppercase.

    Option b, c and d are incorrect. B would be returned if the format mask was 'fmddth Month', and C would be returned if the format mask was 'fmDDspth MONTH'.

98. **What value is returned after executing the following statement?**

    ```
    SELECT NVL2(NULLIF('CODA', 'SID'), 'SPANIEL', 'TERRIER')
    FROM DUAL;
    ```

    (Choose the best answer.)

a) SPANIEL
b) TERRIER
c) NULL
d) None of the above

Answer: a

Explanation:

Option a. The NULLIF function compares its two parameters, and since they are different, the first parameter is returned. The NVL2('CODA', 'SPANIEL','TERRIER') function call returns SPANIEL, since its first parameter is not null.

Option b, c and d are incorrect.

99. **If SYSDATE returns 12-JUL-2009, what Is returned by the following statement?**

```
SELECT DECODE(TO_CHAR(SYSDATE, 'MM'), '02', 'TAX DUE',
'PARTY') FROM DUAL;
```

(Choose the best answer.)

a) TAX DUE
b) PARTY
c) 02
d) None of the above

Answer: b

Explanation:

Option b. The innermost function TO_CHAR(SYSDATE, 'MM') results in the character string '07' being returned. The outer function is DECODE('07','02','TAX DUE','PARTY'). Since '07' is not equal to '02', the else component 'PARTY' is returned.

Option a, c and d are incorrect. A would only be returned if the month component extracted from SYSDATE was '02'.

100. **What result is returned by the following statement?**

```
SELECT COUNT(*) FROM DUAL;
```

(Choose the best answer.)

a) NULL
b) 0
c) 1
d) None of the above

Answer: c

Explanation:

Option c. The DUAL table has one row and one column. The COUNT(*) function returns the number of rows in a table or group.

Option a, b and d are incorrect.

101.   Choose one correct statement regarding group functions.

a)   A. Group functions may only be used when a GROUP BY clause is present.
b)   B. Group functions can operate on multiple rows at a time.
c)   C. Group functions only operate on a single row at a time.
d)   D. Group functions can execute multiple times within a single group.

Answer: b

Explanation:

Option b. By definition, group functions can operate on multiple rows at a time, unlike single-row functions.

Option a, c and d, A group function may be used without a GROUP BY clause. In this case, the entire dataset is operated on as a group. The COUNT function is often executed against an entire table, which behaves as one group. Option d is incorrect. Once a dataset has been partitioned into different groups, any group functions execute once per group.

102.   What value is returned after executing the following statement?

```
SELECT SUM(SALARY) FROM EMPLOYEES;
```

Assume there are ten employee records and each contains a SALARY value of 100, except for one, which has a null value in the SALARY field. (Choose the best answer.)

a)   900
b)   1000
c)   NULL
d)   None of the above

Answer: a

Explanation:

Option a. The SUM aggregate function ignores null values and adds non-null values. Since nine rows contain the SALARY value 100, 900 is returned.

Option b would be returned if SUM(NVL(SALARY,100)) were executed.
Option c is a tempting choice, since regular arithmetic with NULL values returns a NULL result. However, the aggregate functions, except for COUNT(*), ignore NULL values.

103.   4. Which values are returned after executing the following statement?

```
SELECT COUNT(*), COUNT(SALARY) FROM EMPLOYEES;
```

Assume there are ten employee records and each contains a SALARY value of 100, except for one, which has a null value in their SALARY field. (Choose all that apply.)

a) 10 and 10
b) 10 and NULL
c) 10 and 9
d) None of the above

Answer: c

Explanation:

Option c. COUNT(*) considers all rows, including those with NULL values, while COUNT(SALARY) only considers the non-null rows.

Option a, b and d are incorrect.

104.   **What value is returned after executing the following statement?**

```
SELECT AVG(NVL(SALARY,100)) FROM EMPLOYEES;
```

Assume there are eleven employee records and each contains a SALARY value of 100, except for one employee, who has a null value in the SALARY field. (Choose the best answer.)

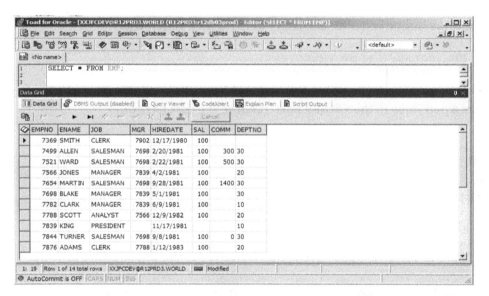

a) NULL
b) 90
c) 100
d) None of the above

Answer: c

Explanation:

Option c. The NVL function converts the one NULL value into 100. Thereafter, the average function adds the SALARY values and obtains 1000. Dividing this by the number of records returns 100.

Option a, b, and d. Option b would be returned if AVG(NVL(SALARY,0)) were selected. It is interesting to note that if AVG(SALARY) were selected, 100 would have also been returned, since the AVG function would sum the non-null values and divide the total by the number of rows with non-null SALARY values. So AVG(SALARY) would be calculated as: 1000/10=100.

Illustration:

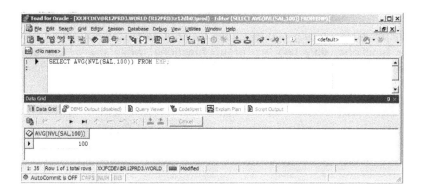

105.   What value is returned after executing the following statement?

```
SELECT SUM((AVG(LENGTH(NVL(SALARY,0)))))
FROM EMPLOYEES
GROUP BY SALARY;
```

Assume there are ten employee records and each contains a SALARY value of 100, except for one, which has a null value in the SALARY field. (Choose the best answer.)

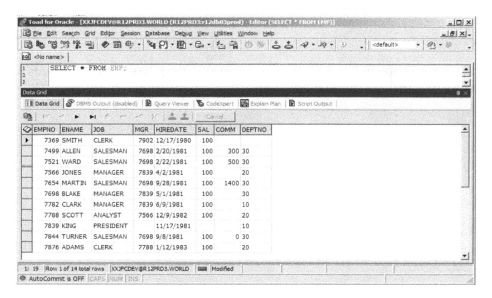

a) An error is returned
b) 3
c) 4
d) None of the above

Answer: c

Explanation:

Option c. The dataset is segmented by the SALARY column. This creates two groups: one with SALARY values of 100 and the other with a null SALARY value. The average length of SALARY value 100 is 3 for the rows in the first group. The NULL salary value is first converted into the number 0 by the NVL function, and the average length of SALARY is 1. The SUM function operates across the two groups adding the values 3 and 1, returning 4.

Option a seems plausible, since group functions may not be nested more than two levels deep. Although there are four functions, only two are group functions, while the others are single-row functions evaluated before the group functions. Option b would be returned if the expression SUM(AVG(LENGTH(SALARY))) were selected.

Illustration:

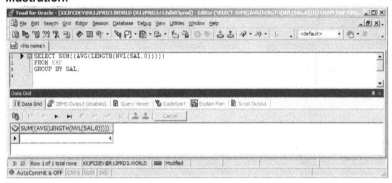

106.   How many rows are returned by the following query?

```
SELECT SUM(SAL), DEPTNO FROM EMP
GROUP BY DEPTNO;
```

Assume there are 13 non-null and 1 null unique DEPARTMENT_ID values. All records have a non-null SALARY value. (Choose the best answer.)

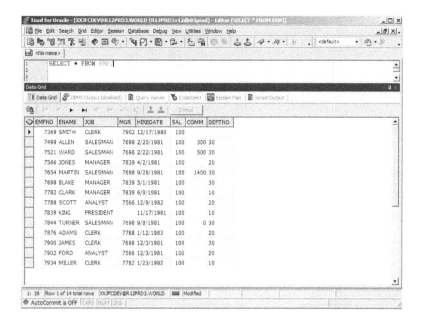

a) 4

b) 11

c) NULL

d) None of the above

Answer: a

Explanation:

Option a. There are 4 distinct DEPARTMENT_ID values. Since this is the grouping attribute, 4 groups are created, including 1 with a null DEPARTMENT_ID value. Therefore 4 rows are returned.

Option b, c and d are incorrect.

Illustration:

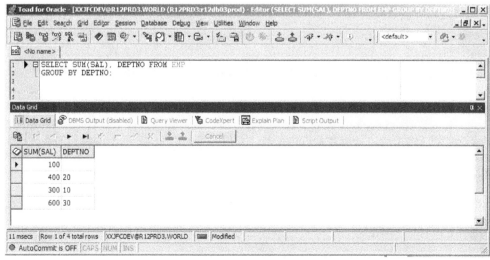

107.   What values are returned after executing the following statement?

```
SELECT JOB_ID, MAX_SALARY FROM JOBS GROUP BY MAX_SALARY;
```

Assume that the JOBS table has ten records with the same JOB_ID value of DBA and the same MAX_SALARY value of 100. (Choose the best answer.)

a) One row of output with the values DBA, 100
b) Ten rows of output with the values DBA, 100
c) An error is returned
d) None of the above

Answer: c

Explanation:

Option c. For a GROUP BY clause to be used, a group function must appear in the SELECT list.

Optin a b and d. These are incorrect, since the statement is syntactically inaccurate and is disallowed by Oracle. Do not mistake the column named MAX_SALARY for the MAX(SALARY) function.

108.   **How many rows of data are returned after executing the following statement?**

```
SELECT DEPTNO, SUM(NVL(SAL,100)) FROM EMP
GROUP BY DEPTNO HAVING SUM(SAL) > 400;
```

Assume the EMP table has ten rows and each contains a SAL value of 100, except for one, which has a null value in the SAL field. The first five rows have a DEPTNO value of 10 while the second group of five rows, which includes the row with a null SAL value, has a DEPTNO value of 20. (Choose the best answer.)

a) Two rows
b) One row
c) Zero rows
d) None of the above

Answer: b

Explanation:

Option b. Two groups are created based on their common DEPTNO values. The group with DEPTNO values of 10 consists of five rows with SAL values of 100 in each of them. Therefore, the SUM(SAL) function returns 500 for this group, and it satisfies the HAVING SUM(SAL) > 400 clause. The group with DEPTNO values of 20 has four rows with SAL values of 100 and one row with a NULL SAL. SUM(SAL) only returns 400 and this group does not satisfy the HAVING clause.

Option a, c and d. Beware of the SUM(NVL(SAL,100)) expression in the SELECT clause. This expression selects the format of the output. It does not restrict or limit the dataset in anyway.

Illustration:
Given:

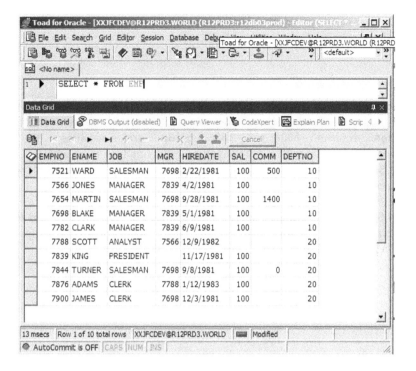

Result:

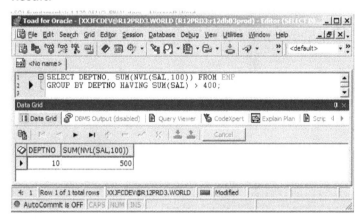

109.   **How many rows of data are returned after executing the following statement?**

```
SELECT DEPTNO, SUM(SAL) FROM EMP GROUP BY DEPTNO
HAVING SUM(NVL(SAL,100)) > 400;
```

Assume the EMP table has ten rows and each contains a SAL value of 100, except for one, which has a null value in the SAL field. The first five rows have a DEPTNO value of 10, while the second five rows, which include the row with a null SAL value, have a DEPTNO value of 20. (Choose the best answer.)

a) Two rows
b) One row
c) Zero rows
d) None of the above

Answer: a

Explanation:

Option a. Two groups are created based on their common DEPTNO values. The group with DEPTNO values of 10 consists of five rows with SAL values of 100 in each of them. Therefore the SUM(NVL(SAL,100)) function returns 500 for this group and satisfies the HAVING SUM(NVL(SAL,100))>400 clause. The group with DEPTNO values of 20 has four rows with SAL values of 100 and one row with a null SAL. SUM(NVL(SAL,100)) returns 500, and this group satisfies the HAVING clause. Therefore, two rows are returned.

Option b, c and d. Although the SELECT clause contains SUM(SAL), which returns 500 and 400 for the two groups, the HAVING clause contains the SUM(NVL(SAL,100)) expression, which specifies the inclusion or exclusion criteria for a group-level row.

Illustration:

Given:

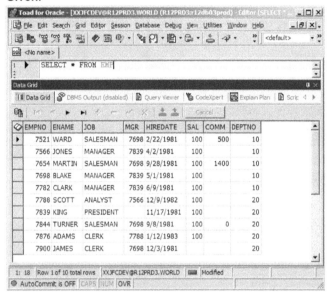

Result

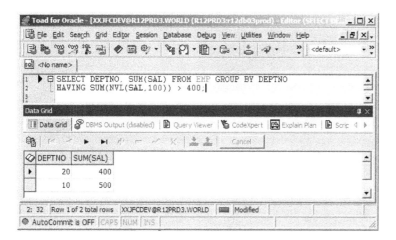

110. The EMP and DEPT tables have two identically named column: DEPTNO. Which of these statements joins these tables based only on common DEPTNO values? (Choose all that apply.)

a) SELECT * FROM EMP NATURAL JOIN DEPT;
b) SELECT * FROM EMP E NATURAL JOIN DEPT D ON
   E.DEPTNO=D.DEPTNO;
c) SELECT * FROM EMP NATURAL JOIN DEPT USING
   (DEPTNO);
d) None of the above

Answer: a

Explanation:

Option a. Performs a pure natural join that implicitly joins the two tables on all columns with identical names, which, in this case, is DEPNO.
Option d. The queries in Option b and Option c incorrectly contain the NATURAL keyword. If this is removed, they will join the DEPT and EMP tables based on the DEPTNO column.

Illustration:
Given:
Table DEPT

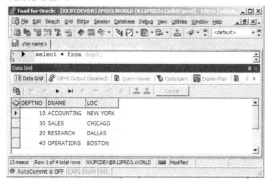

Table EMP

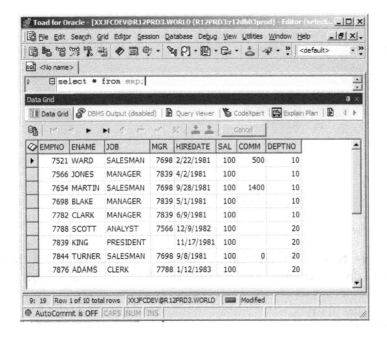

Result:

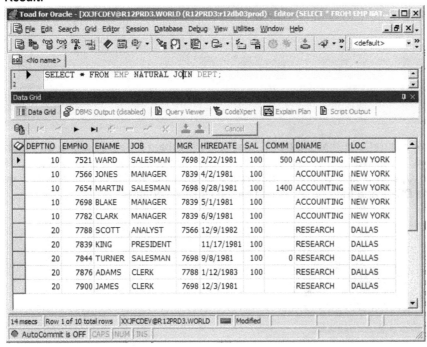

111. The EMP and DEPT tables have one identically named columns: DEPTNO. Which statements join these tables based on column values? (Choose one that does not apply.)

a) SELECT * FROM EMP NATURAL JOIN DEPT;
b) SELECT * FROM EMP JOIN DEPT USING (DEPTNO);
c) SELECT * FROM EMP E JOIN DEPT D ON
   E.DEPTNO=D.DEPTNO;
d) None of the above

Answer: d

Explanation:

Option a and b. These clauses demonstrate different techniques to join the tables on both the DEPTNO.

Option c is incorrect. It will prompt an error.

Illustration:

Option a OUTPUT

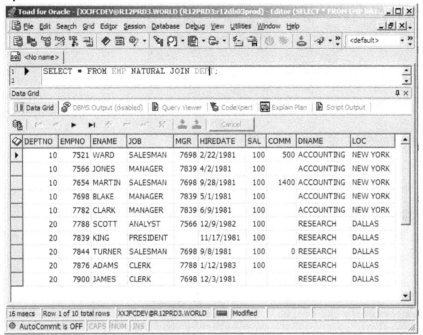

Option b OUTPUT:

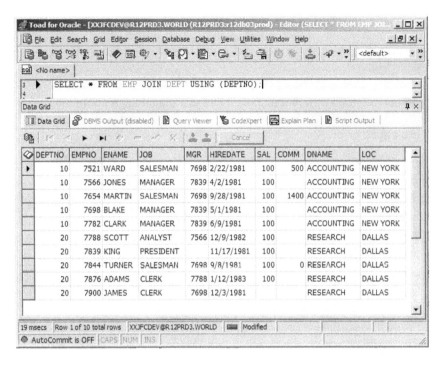

Option c OUTPUT:

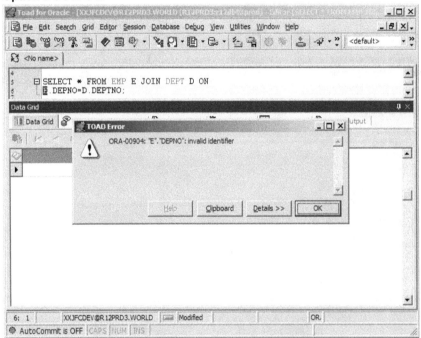

112. Which join is performed by the following query?

```
SELECT E.JOB_ID ,J.JOB_ID FROM EMPLOYEES E
JOIN JOBS J ON (E.SALARY < J.MAX_SALARY);
```

(Choose the best answer.)

a) Equijoin

b) Nonequijoin
c) Cross join
d) Outer join

Answer: b

Explanation:

Option b. The join condition is an expression based on the less than inequality operator. Therefore, this join is a nonequijoin.

Option a, c and d. Option a would be correct if the operator in the join condition expression was an equality operator. The CROSS JOIN keywords or the absence of a join condition would result in Option c being true. Option d would be true if one of the OUTER JOIN clause was used instead of the JOIN . . . ON clause.

113. **Which of the following statements are syntactically correct? (Choose all that apply.)**

a) SELECT * FROM EMP E JOIN DEPT D USING (DEPTNO);
b) SELECT * FROM EMP JOIN DEPT D USING (D.DEPTNO);
c) SELECT D.DEPTNO FROM EMP JOIN DEPT D USING (DEPTNO);
d) None of the above

Answer: a

Explanation:

Option a. This statement demonstrates the correct usage of the JOIN . . . USING clause.

Option b and c. Option b is incorrect because only nonqualified column names are allowed in the brackets after the USING keyword. Option c is incorrect because the column in brackets after the USING keyword cannot be referenced with a qualifier in the SELECT clause.

Illustration:
Option a OUTPUT

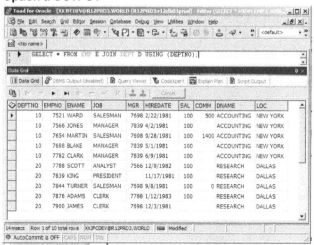

Option b OUTPUT:

Option c OUTPUT:

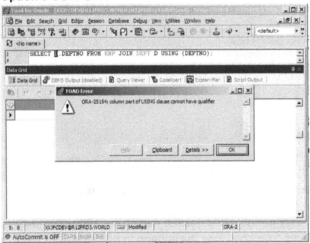

114. **Which of the following statements are syntactically correct? (Choose all that apply.)**

   a) SELECT E.EMPLOYEE_ID, J.JOB_ID PREVIOUS_JOB, E.JOB_ID
      CURRENT_JOB FROM JOB_HISTORY J CROSS JOIN EMPLOYEES E ON
      (J.START_DATE=E.HIRE_DATE);
   b) SELECT E.EMPLOYEE_ID, J.JOB_ID PREVIOUS_JOB, E.JOB_ID
      CURRENT_JOB FROM JOB_HISTORY J JOIN EMPLOYEES E ON
      (J.START_DATE=E.HIRE_DATE);
   c) SELECT E.EMPLOYEE_ID, J.JOB_ID PREVIOUS_JOB, E.JOB_ID
      CURRENT_JOB FROM JOB_HISTORY J OUTER JOIN EMPLOYEES E ON
      (J.START_DATE=E.HIRE_DATE);
   d) None of the above

Answer: b

Explanation:

Option b demonstrates the correct usage of the JOIN . . . ON clause.

Option a is incorrect since the CROSS JOIN clause cannot contain the ON keyword. Option c is incorrect since the OUTER JOIN keywords must be preceded by the LEFT, RIGHT, or FULL keyword.

115. **Choose one correct statement regarding the following query:**

```
SELECT * FROM EMPLOYEES E
JOIN DEPARTMENTS D ON (D.DEPARTMENT_ID=E.DEPARTMENT_ID)
JOIN LOCATIONS L ON (L.LOCATION_ID =D.LOCATION_ID);
```

a) Joining three tables is not permitted.
b) A Cartesian product is generated.
c) The JOIN . . . ON clause may be used for joins between multiple tables.
d) None of the above.

Answer: c

Explanation:

Option c. The JOIN . . . ON clause and the other join clauses may all be used for joins between multiple tables. The JOIN . . . ON and JOIN . . . USING clauses are better suited for N-way table joins.

Option a, b and d. Option a is false, since you may join as many tables as you wish. A Cartesian product is not created, since there are two join conditions and three tables.

116. **How many rows are returned after executing the following statement?**

```
SELECT * FROM REGIONS R1 JOIN REGIONS R2 ON (R1.REGION_
ID=LENGTH(R2.REGION_NAME)/2);
```

The REGIONS table contains the following row data. (Choose the best answer.)

REGION_ID	REGION_NAME
1	Europe
2	Americas
3	Asia
4	Middle East and Africa

a) 2
b) 3
c) 4
d) None of the above

Answer: b

Explanation:

Option b. Three rows are returned. For the row with a REGION_ID value of 2, the REGION_NAME is Asia and half the length of the REGION_NAME is also 2. Therefore this row is returned. The same logic results in the rows with REGION_ID values of 3 and 4 and REGION_NAME values of Europe and Americas being returned.

Option a, c and d are incorrect.

117.   **Choose one correct statement regarding the following query:**

```
SELECT C.COUNTRY_ID
FROM LOCATIONS L RIGHT OUTER JOIN COUNTRIES C
ON (L.COUNTRY_ID=C.COUNTRY_ID) WHERE L.COUNTRY_ID is NULL;
```

a) A. The rows returned represent those countries for which there are no locations.
b) B. The rows returned represent those locations that have no COUNTRY_ID.
c) C. The rows returned represent the COUNTRY_ID values for all the rows in the LOCATIONS table.
d) D. None of the above.

Answer: a

Explanation:

Option a. The right outer join fetches the COUNTRY.COUNTRY_ID values that do not exist in the LOCATIONS table in addition to performing an inner join between the tables. The WHERE clause then eliminates the inner join results. The rows remaining represent those countries for which there are no locations.

Option b, c and d are incorrect.

118.   **Which of the following statements are syntactically correct? (Choose all that apply.)**

a) A. SELECT JH.JOB_ID FROM JOB_HISTORY JH RIGHT OUTER JOIN JOBS J ON JH.JOB_ID=J.JOB_ID
b) B. SELECT JOB_ID FROM JOB_HISTORY JH RIGHT OUTER JOIN JOBS J ON (JH.JOB_ID=J.JOB_ID)
c) C. SELECT JOB_HISTORY.JOB_ID FROM JOB_HISTORY OUTER JOIN JOBS ON JOB_HISTORY.JOB_ID=JOBS.JOB_ID
d) D. None of the above

Answer: a

Explanation:

Option a. This statement demonstrates the correct use of the RIGHT OUTER JOIN . . . ON clause.

The JOB_ID column in the SELECT clause in Option b is not qualified and is therefore ambiguous, since the table from which this column comes is not specified. Option c uses an OUTER JOIN without the keywords LEFT, RIGHT, or FULL.

119.   **If the REGIONS table, which contains 4 rows, is cross joined to the COUNTRIES table, which contains 25 rows, how many rows appear in the final results set? (Choose the best answer.)**

a) 100 rows
b) 4 rows

c) 25 rows
d) None of the above

Answer: a

Explanation:

Option a. The cross join associates every four rows from the REGIONS table 25 times with the rows from the COUNTRIES table, yielding a result set that contains 100 rows.

Option b, c and d are incorrect.

120.   **Consider this generic description of a SELECT statement:**

```
SELECT select_list
FROM table
WHERE condition
GROUP BY expression_1
HAVING expression_2
ORDER BY expression_3 ;
```

Where could subqueries be used? (Choose all correct answers.)

a) select_list
b) table
c) condition
d) expression_1
e) expression_2
f) expression_3

Answer: a

Explanation:

Option a, b, c, and e. Subqueries can be used at all these points.

Option d and f. A subquery cannot be used in the GROUP BY and ORDER BY clauses of a query.

121.   **A query can have a subquery embedded within it. Under what circumstances could there be more than one subquery? (Choose the best answer.)**

a) The outer query can include an inner query. It is not possible to have another query within the inner query.
b) It is possible to embed a single-row subquery inside a multiple-row subquery, but not the other way round.
c) The outer query can have multiple inner queries, but they must not be embedded within each other.
d) Subqueries can be embedded within each other with no practical limitations on depth.

Answer: d

Explanation:

Option d. Subquery nesting can be done to many levels.

Option a and c are incorrect because subqueries can be nested. Option b is incorrect because the number of rows returned is not relevant to nesting subqueries, only to the operators being used.

122.   **Consider this statement:**

```
select employee_id, last_name from employees where
salary > (select avg(salary) from employees);
```

When will the subquery be executed? (Choose the best answer.)

a) It will be executed before the outer query.
b) It will be executed after the outer query.
c) It will be executed concurrently with the outer query.
d) It will be executed once for every row in the EMPLOYEES table.

Answer: a

Explanation:

Option a. The result set of the inner query is needed before the outer query can run.

Option b and c are not possible because the result of the subquery is needed before the parent query can start. Option d is incorrect because the subquery is only run once.

123.   **Consider this statement:**

```
select o.employee_id, o.last_name from employees o where
o.salary > (select avg(i.salary) from employees i
where i.department_id=o.department_id);
```

When will the subquery be executed? (Choose the best answer.)

a) It will be executed before the outer query.
b) It will be executed after the outer query.
c) It will be executed concurrently with the outer query.
d) It will be executed once for every row in the EMPLOYEES table.

Answer: d

Explanation:

D. This is a correlated subquery, which must be run for every row in the table.

A, B, and C. The result of the inner query is dependent on a value from the outer query; it must therefore be run once for every row.

124.   **Consider the following statement:**

```
select ename from emp join dept
on emp.deptno = dept.deptno
where dname='ACCOUNTING';
```

and this statement:

```
select ename from emp where deptno in
(select deptno from dept where dname='ACCOUNTING');
```

What can be said about the two statements? (Choose two correct answers.)

a)   The two statements should generate the same result.
b)   The two statements could generate different results.
c)   The first statement will always run successfully; the second statement will error if there are two departments with DNAME 'ACCOUNTING'.
d)   Both statements will always run successfully, even if there are two departments with DNAME 'ACCOUNTING'.

Answer: a, d

Explanation:

Option a and d. The two statements will deliver the same result, and neither will fail if the name is duplicated.

Option b is incorrect because the statements are functionally identical, though syntactically different. Option c is incorrect because the comparison operator used, IN, can handle a multiple-row subquery.

Illustration:

Statement 1:

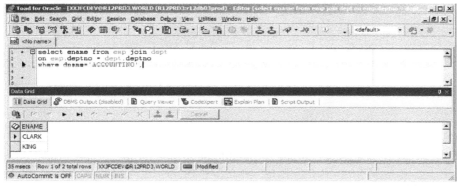

Statement 2:

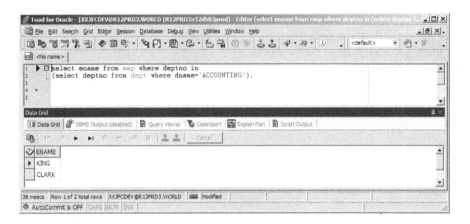

125. **What are the distinguishing characteristics of a scalar subquery? (Choose two correct answers.)**

    a) A scalar subquery returns one row.
    b) A scalar subquery returns one column.
    c) A scalar subquery cannot be used in the SELECT LIST of the parent query.
    d) A scalar subquery cannot be used as a correlated subquery.

    Answer: a, b

    Explanation:

    Option a and b are scalar subquery can be defined as a query that returns a single value.

    Option c is incorrect because a scalar subquery is the only subquery that can be used in the SELECT LIST.

    Option d is incorrect because scalar subqueries can be correlated.

126. **Which comparison operator cannot be used with multiple-row subqueries? (Choose the best answer.)**

    a) ALL
    b) ANY
    c) IN
    d) All the above can be used

    Answer: d

    Explanation:

    Option d. ALL, ANY, IN, and NOT IN are the multiple-row comparison operators.

    Option a, b and c. All of these can be used.

127. **Consider this statement:**

```
select last_name, (select count(*) from departments) from
employees
where salary = (select salary from employees);
```

What is wrong with it? (Choose the best answer.)

a) Nothing is wrong—the statement should run without error.
b) The statement will fail because the subquery in the SELECT list references a table that is not listed in the FROM clause.
c) The statement will fail if the conditional subquery returns more than one row.
d) The statement will run but is extremely inefficient because of the need to run the second subquery once for every row in EMPLOYEES.

Answer: c

Explanation:

Option c. The equality operator requires a single-row subquery, and the conditional subquery could return several rows.

Option a is incorrect because the statement will fail in all circumstances except the unlikely case where there is zero or one employee.

Option b is incorrect because this is not a problem; there need be no relationship between the source of data for the inner and outer queries.

Option d is incorrect because the subquery will only run once; it is not a correlated subquery.

Illustration:

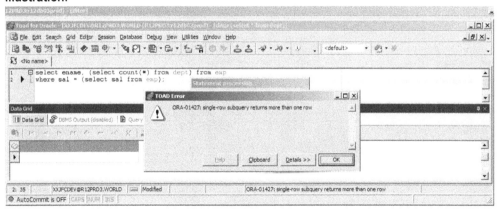

128.   **Which of the following statements are equivalent? (Choose two answers.)**

a) select empno from emp where sal < all
    (select sal from emp where deptno=10);

b) select empno from emp where sal <

(select min(sal) from emp where deptno=10);

c) select empno from emp where sal
   not >= any (select sal from emp where deptno=10);

d) select empno from emp e join dept d on e.deptno=d.deptno where e.sal <
   (select min(sal) from emp) and d.deptno=10;

Answer: a

Explanation:

Option a and b are identical.

Option c is logically the same as Option a and b but syntactically is not possible; it will give an error.

Option d will always return no rows, because it asks for all employees who have a salary lower than all employees. This is not an error but can never return any rows. The filter on DEPARTMENTS is not relevant.

Illustation:

Option a

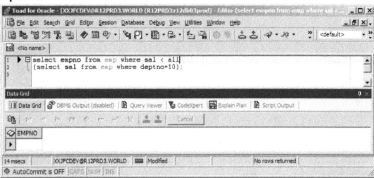

Option b

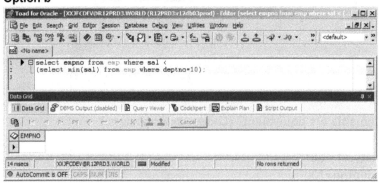

Option c

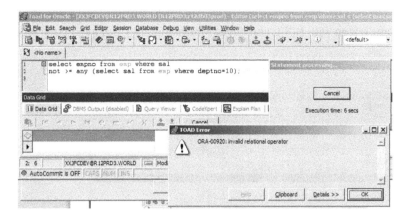

Option d

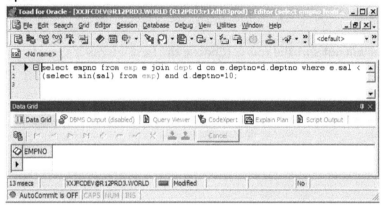

129. **Consider this statement, which is intended to prompt for an employee's name and then find all employees who have the same job as the first employee:**

```
select ename,empno from emp where job =
(select job from emp where ename = '&Name');
```

What would happen if a value were given for &Name that did not match with any row in EMPLOYEES? (Choose the best answer.)

a) The statement would fail with an error.
b) The statement would return every row in the table.
c) The statement would return no rows.
d) The statement would return all rows where JOB_ID is NULL.

Answer: c

Explanation:

Option c. If a subquery returns NULL, then the comparison will also return NULL, meaning that no rows will be retrieved.

Option a is incorrect because this would not cause an error.

Option b is incorrect because a comparison with NULL will return nothing, not everything.

Option d is incorrect because a comparison with NULL can never return anything, not even other NULLs.

Illustration:
After running the SQL Script.

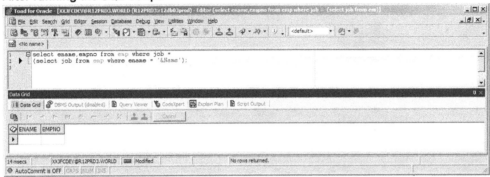

130.   Which of these set operators will not sort the rows? (Choose the best answer.)

a) INTERSECT
b) MINUS
c) UNION
d) UNION ALL

Answer: d

Explanation:

Option d. UNION ALL returns rows in the order that they are delivered by the queries that make up the compound query.

Option a, b and c. INTERSECT, MINUS, and UNION all use sorting as part of their execution.

131.   Which of these operators will remove duplicate rows from the final result? (Choose one that does not apply.)

a) INTERSECT
b) MINUS
c) UNION
d) UNION ALL

Answer: d

Explanation:

Option d. UNION ALL returns all rows, duplicates included.

Option a, b and c. INTERSECT, MINUS, and UNION all remove duplicate rows.

132.   If a compound query contains both a MINUS and an INTERSECT operator, which will be applied first? (Choose the best answer.)

a) The INTERSECT, because INTERSECT has a higher precedence than MINUS.
b) The MINUS, because MINUS has a higher precedence than INTERSECT.
c) The precedence is determined by the order in which they are specified.
d) It is not possible for a compound query to include both MINUS and INTERSECT.

Answer: c

Explanation:

Option c. All set operators have equal precedence, so the precedence is determined by the sequence in which they occur.

Option a and b are incorrect because set operators have equal precedence—though this may change in future releases.

Option d is incorrect because many set operators can be used in one compound query.

133.   There are four rows in the REGIONS table. Consider the following statements and choose how many rows will be returned for each: 0, 4, 8, or 16.

a) select * from regions union select * from regions
b) select * from regions union all select * from regions
c) select * from regions minus select * from regions
d) select * from regions intersect select * from regions

Answer: a

Explanation:

A = 4; B = 8; C = 0; D = 4.

Note that 16 is not used; that would be the result of a Cartesian product query.

134.   Consider this compound query:

```
select empno, hiredate from emp
union all
select emp_id,hiredate,fired from ex_emp;
```

The columns EMP.EMPNO and EX_EMP.EMP_ID are integer; the column EMP.HIRED is timestamp; the columns EX_EMP.HIRED and EX_EMP.FIRED are date. Why will the statement fail? (Choose the best answer.)

a) Because the columns EMPNO and EMP_ID have different names
b) Because the columns EMP.HIRED and EX_EMP.HIRED are different data types
c) Because there are two columns in the first query and three columns in the second query
d) For all the reasons above

Answer: c

Explanation:

Option c. Every query in a compound query must return the same number of columns.

Option a is incorrect because the columns can have different names.

Option b is incorrect because the two columns are of the same data type group, which is all that was required. It therefore follows that Option b and d are also incorrect.

Illustration:
When running the SQL Script.

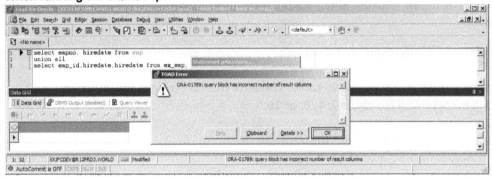

135.   **Which line of this statement will cause it to fail? (Choose the best answer.)**

a)   select ename, hired from current_staff
b)   order by ename
c)   minus
d)   select ename, hired from current staff
e)   where deptno=10
f)   order by ename;

Answer: b

Explanation:

Option b. You cannot use ORDER BY for one query of a compound query; you may only place a single
    ORDER BY clause at the end.

Option a, c, d, e, and f. All these lines are legal.

Illustration:
USING THE GIVEN SQL SCRIPT

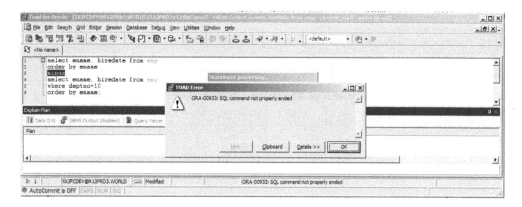

AFTER REMOVING LINE 2 OF THE SQL SCRIPT

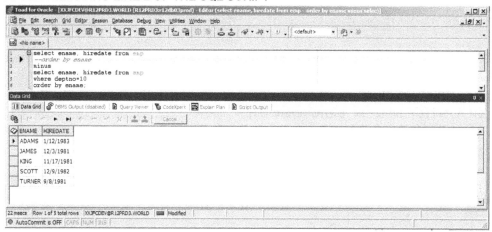

136.   **Study this statement:**

```
select ename from emp union all select ename from ex_emp;
```

In what order will the rows be returned? (Choose the best answer.)

a) The rows from each table will be grouped and within each group will be sorted on ENAME.
b) The rows from each table will be grouped but not sorted.
c) The rows will not be grouped, but will all be sorted on ENAME.
d) The rows will be neither grouped nor sorted.

Answer: b

Explanation:

Option b. The rows from each query will be grouped together, but there will be no sorting.

Option a is not possible with any syntax.

Option c is incorrect because that would be the result of a UNION, not a UNION ALL.

Option d is incorrect because UNION ALL will return the rows from each query grouped together.

Illustration:

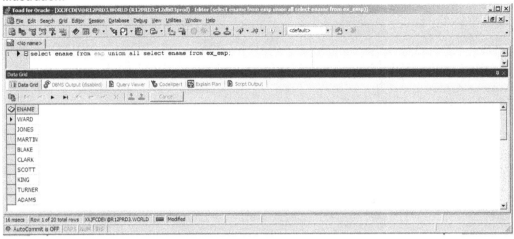

137.   **The STATE table has the following constraints (the constraint status is shown in parentheses):**

Primary key **pk_state** (enabled)
Foreign key **COUNTRY** table: **fk_state** (enabled)
Check constraint **ck_cnt_code** (disabled)
Check constraint **ck_st_code** (enabled)
Not null constraint **nn_st_name** (enabled)

You execute the following SQL:

CREATE TABLE STATE_NEW AS SELECT * FROM STATE;

How many constraints will there be in the new table?

a) 0
b) 1
c) 3
d) 5
e) 2

Answer: b

Explanation:

When you create a table using CTAS (CREATE TABLE AS SELECT), only the NOT NULL constraints are copied.

138.   **Which line of code has an error?**

```
1 CREATE TABLE FRUITS_VEGETABLES
2 (FRUIT_TYPE VARCHAR2,
3 FRUIT_NAME CHAR (20),
4 QUANTITY NUMBER);
```

a) 1
b) 2
c) 3
d) 4

Answer: b

Explanation:

A VARCHAR2 datatype should always specify the maximum length of the column.

Illustration:

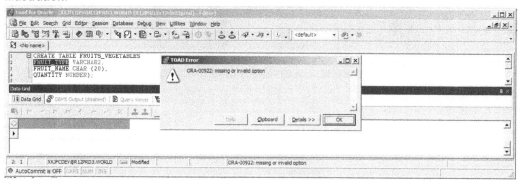

139.   Which statement successfully adds a new column, ORDER_DATE, to the table ORDERS?

a)   ALTER TABLE ORDERS ADD COLUMN ORDER_DATE DATE;
b)   ALTER TABLE ORDERS ADD ORDER_DATE (DATE);
c)   ALTER TABLE ORDERS ADD ORDER_DATE DATE;
d)   ALTER TABLE ORDERS NEW COLUMN ORDER_DATE TYPE DATE;

Answer: c

Explanation:

The correct statement is C. When adding only one column, the column definition doesn't need to be enclosed in parentheses.

Illustration:
Option c

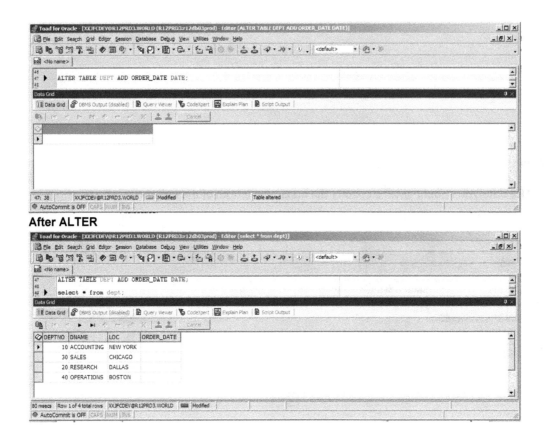

After ALTER

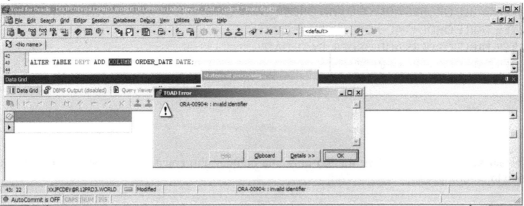

Option a

Option b

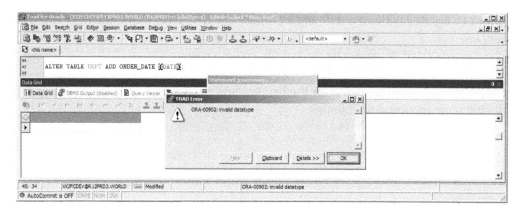

Option d

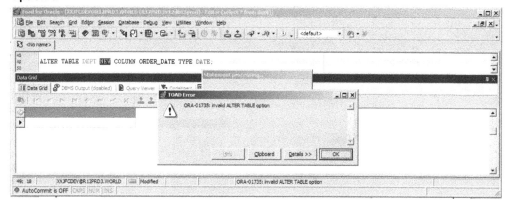

140. **What are the special characters allowed in a table name? (Choose all that apply.)**

a) &
b) !
c) @
d) $

Answer: a

Explanation:

D. Only three special characters ($, _, and #) are allowed in table names along with letters and numbers.

141. **Consider the following statement:**

CREATE TABLE MY_TABLE (
1ST_COLUMN NUMBER,
2ND_COLUMN VARCHAR2 (20));

Which of the following best describes this statement?

a) Tables cannot be created without a defining a primary key. The table definition here is missing the primary key.
b) The reserved word COLUMN cannot be part of the column name.
c) The column names are invalid.
d) There is no maximum length specified for the first column definition. You must always specify a length for character and numeric columns.

Answer: c

Explanation:

All identifiers (column names, table names, and so on) must begin with an alphabetic character. An identifier can contain alphabetic characters, numbers, and the special characters $, #, and _.

Illustration:

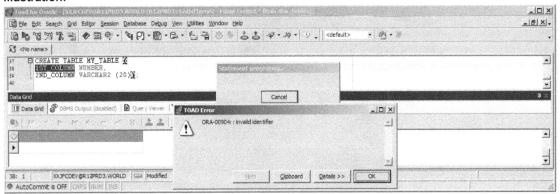

142.   Which dictionary view would you query to list only the tables you own?

a) ALL_TABLES
b) DBA_TABLES
c) USER_TABLES
d) USR_TABLES

Answer: c

Explanation:

Option c. The USER_TABLES view provides information on the tables owned by the user who has logged on that session.

Option a. ALL_TABLES will have the tables owned by you as well as the tables to which you have access.

Option b. DBA_TABLES will have all the tables in the database

Option d. USR_TABLES is not a valid dictionary view.

143.   The EMP table has six rows. You issue the following command:

ALTER TABLE EMP ADD UPDATE_DT DATE DEFAULT SYSDATE;

Which of the following is correct?

a) A new column, UPDATE_DT, is added to the EMP table, and its contents for the existing rows are NULL.
b) Since the table is not empty, you cannot add a new column.
c) The DEFAULT value cannot be provided if the table has rows.
d) A new column, UPDATE_DT, is added to EMP and is populated with the current system date and time.

Answer: d

Explanation:

When a default value is specified in the new column added, the column values for the existing rows are populated with the default value. If you include the NOT NULL constraint with the DEFAULT value, only the dictionary is updated.

Illustration:
BEFORE ALTER

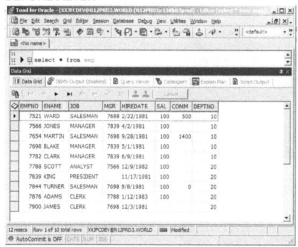

USING ALTER TABLE

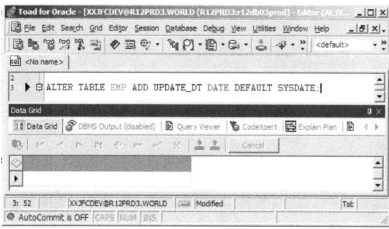

AFTER ALTER

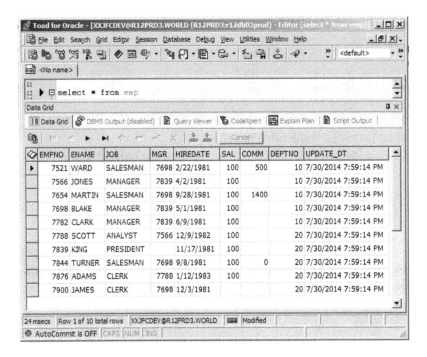

144.   The EMP table has the following data:

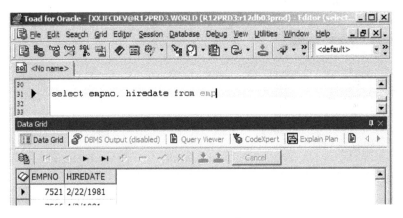

What will be result of the following query?

SELECT hiredate+1 FROM EMP WHERE empno = 7521;

a) 2/23/1981
b) 25-JAN-01
c) N-02
d) None of the above

Answer: a

Explanation:

In date arithmetic, adding 1 is equivalent to adding 24 hours. To add 6 hours to a date value with time, add 0.25.

Illustration:

145. What is the default length of a CHAR datatype column if no length is specified in the table definition?

a) 256
b) 1,000
c) 64
d) 1
e) You must always specify a length for CHAR columns.

Answer: d

Explanation:

If you do not specify a length for a CHAR datatype column, the default length of 1 is assumed.

146. Which statement will remove the column UPDATE_DT from the table STATE?

a) ALTER TABLE STATE DROP COLUMN UPDATE_DT;
b) ALTER TABLE STATE REMOVE COLUMN UPDATE_DT;
c) DROP COLUMN UPDATE_DT FROM STATE;
d) ALTER TABLE STATE SET UNUSED COLUMN UPDATE_DT;
e) You cannot drop a column from the table.

Answer: a

Explanation:

You can use the DROP COLUMN clause with the ALTER TABLE statement to drop a column. There is no separate DROP COLUMN statement or a REMOVE clause in the ALTER TABLE statement. The SET UNUSED clause is used to mark the column as unused. This column can be dropped later using the DROP UNUSED COLUMNS clause.

147. Which actions are allowed on a table that is marked as read-only? (Choose all that apply.)

a) Truncating a table
b) Inserting new data
c) Dropping a constraint
d) Dropping an index
e) Dropping a table

Answer: c, d, e

Explanation:

All actions that do not modify the data in the table are permitted on a read-only table. The actions of creating/dropping a constraint, creating/dropping an index, and dropping a table are allowed. Though truncating is a DDL action, it is not permitted since the data in the table is affected.

148. Which of the following statements will create a primary key for the CITY table with the columns STATE_CD and CITY_CD?

    a) CREATE PRIMARY KEY ON CITY (STATE_CD, CITY_CD);
    b) CREATE CONSTRAINT PK_CITY PRIMARY KEY ON CITY (STATE_CD, CITY_CD);
    c) ALTER TABLE CITY ADD CONSTRAINT PK_CITY PRIMARY KEY (STATE_CD, CITY_CD);
    d) ALTER TABLE CITY ADD PRIMARY KEY (STATE_CD, CITY_CD);

Answer: c

Explanation:

The ALTER TABLE statement is used to create and remove constraints. CREATE PRIMARY KEY and CREATE CONSTRAINT are invalid statements. A constraint is always added to an existing table using the ALTER TABLE statement.

149. Which of the following check constraints will raise an error? (Choose all that apply.)

    a) CONSTRAINT ck_gender CHECK (gender IN ('M', 'F'))
    b) CONSTRAINT ck_old_order CHECK (order_date > (SYSDATE - 30))
    c) CONSTRAINT ck_vendor CHECK (vendor_id IN (SELECT vendor_id FROM vendors))
    d) CONSTRAINT ck_profit CHECK (gross_amt > net_amt)

Answer: b, c

Explanation:

Check constraints cannot reference the SYSDATE function or other tables.

150. Consider the datatypes DATE, TIMESTAMP (TS), TIMESTAMP WITH LOCAL TIME ZONE (TSLTZ), INTERVAL YEAR TO MONTH (IY2M), and INTERVAL DAY TO SECOND (ID2S). Which operations is not allowed by Oracle Database 11g? (Choose all that apply.)

    a) TSLTZ–DATE
    b) TSLTZ+IY2M
    c) TS*5
    d) ID2S/2

Answer: a

Explanation:

You cannot add two DATE datatypes, but you can subtract to find the difference in days. Multiplication and division operators are permitted only on INTERVAL datatypes. When adding or subtracting INTERVAL datatypes, both INTERVAL datatypes should be of the same category.

151. A constraint is created with the DEFERRABLE INITIALLY IMMEDIATE clause. What does this mean?

a) Constraint checking is done only at commit time.
b) Constraint checking is done after each SQL statement is executed, but you can change this behavior by specifying SET CONSTRAINTS ALL DEFERRED.
c) Existing rows in the table are immediately checked for constraint violation.
d) The constraint is immediately checked in a DML operation, but subsequent constraint verification is done at commit time.

Answer: b

Explanation:

DEFERRABLE specifies that the constraint can be deferred using the SET CONSTRAINTS command. INITIALLY IMMEDIATE specifies that the constraint's default behavior is to validate the constraint for each SQL statement executed.

152. What is the default precision for fractional seconds in a TIMESTAMP datatype column?

a) 0
b) 2
c) 6
d) 9

Answer: c

Explanation:

The default precision is 6 digits. The precision can range from 0 to 9.

153. Which datatype shows the time-zone information along with the date value?

a) TIMESTAMP
b) TIMESTAMP WITH LOCAL TIME ZONE
c) TIMESTAMP WITH TIME ZONE
d) DATE

Answer: c

Explanation:

Only TIMESTAMP WITH TIME ZONE stores the time-zone information as a displacement from UTC. TIMESTAMP WITH LOCAL TIME ZONE adjusts the time to the database's time zone before storing it.

154. You have a large job that will load many thousands of rows into your ORDERS table. To speed up the loading process, you want to temporarily stop enforcing the foreign key constraint FK_ORDERS. Which of the following statements will satisfy your requirement?

   a) ALTER CONSTRAINT FK_ORDERS DISABLE;
   b) ALTER TABLE ORDERS DISABLE FOREIGN KEY FK_ORDERS;
   c) ALTER TABLE ORDERS DISABLE CONSTRAINT FK_ORDERS;
   d) ALTER TABLE ORDERS DISABLE ALL CONSTRAINTS;

   Answer: c

   Explanation

   You can disable a constraint by specifying its constraint name. You may enable the constraint after the load and avoid the constraint checking while enabling using the ALTER TABLE ORDERS MODIFY CONSTRAINT FK_ORDERS ENABLE NOVALIDATE; command.

155. You are connected to the database as user JOHN. You need to rename a table named NORDERS to NEW_ORDERS, owned by SMITH. Consider the following two statements:

   1. RENAME SMITH.NORDERS TO NEW_ORDERS;
   2. ALTER TABLE SMITH.NORDERS RENAME TO NEW_ORDERS;

   Which of the following is correct?

   a) Statement 1 will work; statement 2 will not.
   b) Statements 1 and 2 will work.
   c) Statement 1 will not work; statement 2 will work.
   d) Statements 1 and 2 will not work.

   Answer: c

   Explanation

   RENAME can be used to rename objects owned by the user. ALTER TABLE should be used to rename tables owned by another user. To do so, you must have the ALTER privilege on the table or the ALTER ANY TABLE privilege.

156. Tom executed the following SQL statement.

   create table xx (n number, x long, y clob);

   Choose the best option.

   a) A table named xx will be created.
   b) Single-character column names are not allowed in table definitions.
   c) When using the LONG datatype, other LOB datatypes cannot be used in table definitions.

d) One of the datatypes used in the column definition needs the size specified.

Answer: a

Explanation:

The table will be created without error. A table cannot have more than one LONG column, but LONG and multiple LOB columns can exist together. If a LONG or LONG RAW column is defined, another LONG or LONG RAW column cannot be used.

Illustration:
CREATE TABLE

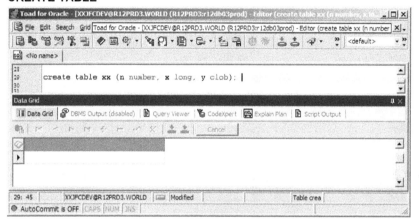

DESCRIBE TABLE

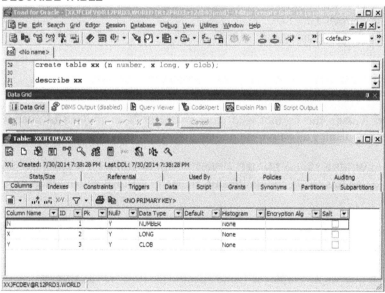

157. **Considering EMP Table has the following data.**

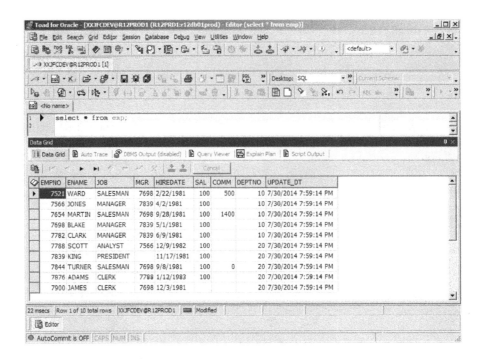

Which of the following SQL statement that will display all Employee with "W" as the first letter of ENAME?

a) SELECT * FROM EMP WHERE ENAME = 'W';
b) SELECT * FROM EMP WHERE ENAME = "W%";
c) SELECT * FROM EMP WHERE ENAME LIKE 'W';
d) SELECT * FROM EMP WHERE ENAME LIKE 'W%';

Answer: d

Explanation:
Option d is the correct answer. It uses the correct wild card character % in replace of succeeding character after letter W which means display all employee names that starts with letter W.

Option b will have an error due to WHERE clause ENAME = "W%". Double-Quote (") is special character in Oracle and it does not allow to use to specify constant value clause in WHERE statement instead use single-quote (').

Option a does not have an error but it does not display all employee name that starts with letter W. The query means, display all employee name letter W.

Option c does not have an error. It queries all Employee name specific to letter "W" as ENAME.

Illustration:
Option a

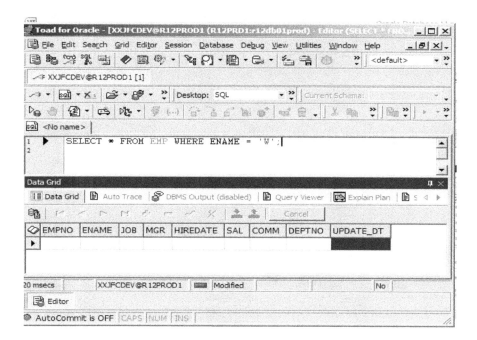

Option b

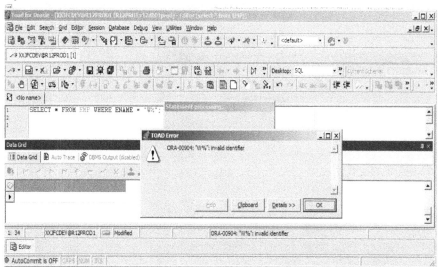

Option c

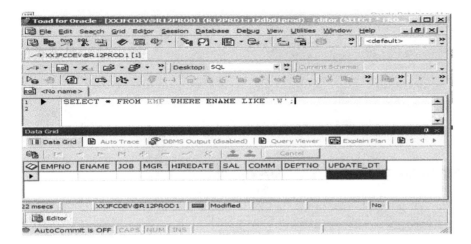

Option d

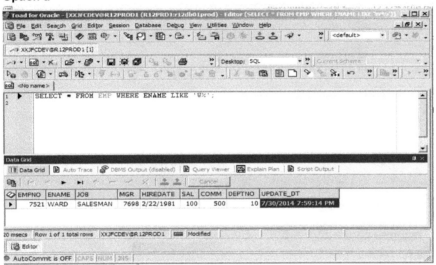

www.ingramcontent.com/pod-product-compliance
Lightning Source LLC
Chambersburg PA
CBHW080428060326
40689CB00019B/4423